Daily Coding Problem

Alex Miller and Lawrence Wu

Copyright © 2019, Alex Miller and Lawrence Wu

All rights reserved. No part of this book may be reproduced in any form or by any electronic or mechanical means, including information storage and retrieval systems, without permission in writing from the publisher, except in the case of brief quotations embodied in critical reviews and certain other noncommercial uses permitted by copyright law. For more information, email the authors at founders@dailycoding-problem.com.

SECOND EDITION

ISBN 978-1-7932966-3-4

Printed in the United States of America

Cover Design by Irene Zou

10 9 8 7 6 5 4 3 2 1

Alex: For Mom, Dad, Jordan, Hannah, and Zaddy

Lawrence: For Mama and Papa

Contents

Contents   **5**

I   Data Structures   **17**

1   Arrays   **19**
     1.1   Get product of all other elements   20
     1.2   Locate smallest window to be sorted   22
     1.3   Calculate maximum subarray sum   24
     1.4   Find number of smaller elements to the right   26

2   Strings   **29**
     2.1   Find anagram indices   29
     2.2   Generate palindrome pairs   32
     2.3   Print zigzag form   34
     2.4   Determine smallest rotated string   36

3   Linked Lists   **41**
     3.1   Reverse linked list   42
     3.2   Add two linked lists that represent numbers   44
     3.3   Rearrange a linked list to alternate high-low   46
     3.4   Find intersecting nodes of linked lists   48

4   Stacks and Queues   **51**
     4.1   Implement a max stack   53
     4.2   Determine whether brackets are balanced   54
     4.3   Compute maximum of k-length subarrays   56
     4.4   Reconstruct array using +/- signs   59

5   Hash Tables   **63**
     5.1   Implement an LRU cache   65
     5.2   Cut brick wall   68

CONTENTS

    5.3   Implement a sparse array 70

6 Trees 73
    6.1   Count unival trees 75
    6.2   Reconstruct tree from pre-order and in-order traversals 79
    6.3   Evaluate arithmetic tree 81
    6.4   Get tree level with minimum sum 83

7 Binary Search Trees 85
    7.1   Find floor and ceiling 87
    7.2   Convert sorted array to BST 88
    7.3   Construct all BSTs with n nodes 90

8 Tries 93
    8.1   Implement autocomplete system 95
    8.2   Create PrefixMapSum class 98
    8.3   Find Maximum XOR of element pairs 101

9 Heaps 105
    9.1   Compute the running median 107
    9.2   Find most similar websites 109
    9.3   Generate regular numbers 111
    9.4   Build a Huffman tree 113

10 Graphs 119
    10.1   Determine if a cycle exists 122
    10.2   Remove edges to create even trees 124
    10.3   Create stepword chain 126
    10.4   Beat Snakes and Ladders 128
    10.5   Topological sort 130

11 Advanced Data Structures 133
    11.1   Fenwick tree 134
    11.2   Disjoint-set data structure 137
    11.3   Bloom filter 140

II Algorithms 143

12 Recursion 145
    12.1   Tower of Hanoi 146
    12.2   Implement regular expressions 149
    12.3   Find array extremes efficiently 151
    12.4   Play Nim 154

CONTENTS

13 Dynamic Programming — 157
- 13.1 Number of ways to climb a staircase 160
- 13.2 Number of ways to decode a string 162
- 13.3 Painting houses 164

14 Backtracking — 167
- 14.1 Compute flight itinerary 169
- 14.2 Solve Sudoku 171
- 14.3 Count Android unlock combinations 174

15 Sorting and Searching — 179
- 15.1 Dutch flag problem 181
- 15.2 Pancake sort 183
- 15.3 Efficiently sort a billion integers 185
- 15.4 Find minimum element in rotated sorted array 186

16 Pathfinding — 189
- 16.1 Dijkstra's algorithm 190
- 16.2 Bellman-Ford 193
- 16.3 Floyd-Warshall 195

17 Bit Manipulation — 199
- 17.1 Find element that appears once in list 201
- 17.2 Implement division without / or * operators 202
- 17.3 Compute longest consecutive string of ones in binary 204
- 17.4 Find n^{th} sevenish number 205

18 Randomized Algorithms — 209
- 18.1 Pick random element from infinite stream 210
- 18.2 Shuffle deck of cards 212
- 18.3 Markov chain 215

19 Advanced Algorithms — 219
- 19.1 Rabin-Karp 220
- 19.2 Hierholzer's algorithm 224
- 19.3 A^* search 227

III Applications — 235

20 Applications — 237
- 20.1 Ghost 238
- 20.2 Connect 4 241
- 20.3 Cryptarithmetic 247

20.4 Cheapest itinerary 251
20.5 Alien dictionary 254
20.6 Prime numbers 256
20.7 Crossword puzzles 259
20.8 UTF-8 encodings 263
20.9 Blackjack 265

IV Design   271

21 Data Structure Design   273
21.1 Dictionary with time key 274
21.2 Queue with fixed-length array 278
21.3 Quack 282

22 System Design   287
22.1 Crawl Wikipedia 288
22.2 Design a hit counter 293
22.3 What happens when you visit a URL? 296

Glossary   299

About the authors

Alex Miller is a software engineer who has interviewed hundreds of candidates on behalf of Yelp, Pinterest, and Intuit. He currently works as an expert interviewer at Karat. He has extensive experience teaching algorithms, data structures, and mathematics. Alex holds a degree in mathematics from Wesleyan University.

Lawrence Wu is a software engineer who has worked at Google, Twitter, and Yelp and has gained deep insight into each company's hiring practices. Most recently, he has worked at Lyft on their self-driving division. Lawrence holds a degree in computer science from the University of Toronto.

About this book

Hello, and thanks for purchasing this book!

You may have bought this book because you are studying for an upcoming interview. Or possibly you anticipate having a coding interview in the future. Or perhaps you are simply interested in improving your knowledge of algorithms and data structures by working through a set of problems! Whatever your use case, we hope you enjoy it.

The questions in this book have been chosen with practicality, clarity, and self-improvement in mind. Each one is based on a real question that was asked recently by top tech companies. The problems and explanations were then carefully edited so that each one communicates a key idea that you can apply more generally. Finally, we have organized these problems into chapters by topic, to ensure that you can methodically build up your skills in specific areas.

At the beginning of each chapter we provide a crash course on the topic that follows, but this book is no substitute for years of coding experience or a course in computer science. As such, we assume that readers have experience with at least one programming language, and have a basic familiarity with concepts such as graphs, recursion, and hash tables.

The structure of this book is as follows. First, we introduce you to the most essential data structures that pop up in coding interviews, such as linked lists, arrays, strings, and hash tables. For each data structure, we offer a refresher on its advantages and disadvantages, the time and space complexities of its operations, its implementation, and what themes and key words to look for in order to recognize it.

Next, we take a tour through a series of must-know algorithms, including dynamic programming, backtracking, sorting, and searching. At the start of each chapter, we discuss when it is a good idea to use each algorithm, and walk through a simple example to describe step by step how it is performed. We examine patterns one can identify to figure out which algorithm to apply in a given problem, and finally we look at a few specialized algorithms that require combining multiple approaches.

Third, we present a set of more advanced problems that require you to use the preceding data structures and algorithms in novel ways in order to solve real-world applications. From deriving a perfect blackjack strategy to deciphering an alien dictionary, these questions are designed to challenge you and widen your understanding of what can be achieved with the right concepts and implementation.

Lastly, we address the topic of design. Interviewers like to gauge the ability of candidates to understand tradeoffs between different approaches. As a result, it is not uncommon to see problems with time and space constraints that require formulating novel data structures. It has also become increasingly frequent for candidates to be asked to design a high-level system that meets a particular need. Our final chapters on data structure and system design walk through each of these question types, respectively, and provide a general strategy for approaching similar problems in the future.

Before you jump in, we offer some general advice for working through the problems.

1. First, really try to solve each problem, even if it seems challenging, and even if you aren't sure where to begin! Look for key words in the question, and write out some pseudocode to get things started. Use the topic groupings to your advantage: review the chapter introduction to see how a particular data structure or algorithm may be relevant. This process of brainstorming and engaging with the question will help to build your problem solving muscle memory.

2. After giving the problem your best shot, read through the solution, looking for not just how the algorithm works but why. What are the core concepts, and to what other problems might they apply? About an hour later, and then a week after, try to implement it again, this time without the solution.

3. Finally, stay positive! Many of these concepts are challenging, and without

practice these data structures and algorithms may not seem intuitive. For example, dynamic programming, a now-common technique, was first developed by top mathematicians during the Cold War to optimize military operations! Rather than trying to understand it all at once, put aside some time each day to work through one or two problems, and let the material sink in gradually.

Good luck!

Part I

Data Structures

1

Arrays

Arrays are without a doubt the most fundamental data structure in computer science. Under the hood, an array is represented as a fixed-size, contiguous block of memory with $\mathcal{O}(1)$ time to store and access an element. Because of this efficiency, many other data structures frequently use arrays for their implementation, such as strings, stacks, queues, and hash tables.

You can picture an array as a bounded row of labeled containers, starting at 0, where you can quickly put items in, take them out, or look up a value from an index (or label).

| 0 | 1 | 2 | 3 | 4 | 5 | 6 | 7 |

For example, in the diagram above, we have an array of length 8. We can set and get the value associated with the third index in constant time using the following operations:

```
array[2] = 'foo'

x = array[2] # 'foo'
```

However, arrays do have a few limitations. Looking up an element up by value typically requires an entire traversal of the array, unless it is sorted in some way. Deleting an element from an array means that all subsequent elements have to be shifted left by one, leading to an $\mathcal{O}(n)$ time operation. If possible, it is better to overwrite the value. Similarly, inserting an element early in the array requires the rest of the elements to be shifted right, so this should be done sparingly.

Finally, arrays have a fixed bound, which means they may not be suitable for applications where the size of the collection of elements is not known ahead of time. In an interview setting, you should be careful of off-by-one errors that lead to trying to access an element outside the range of the array.

Python does not have native support for arrays; typically, you'll use the `list` data structure, which dynamically resizes under the hood. What this means is that to you, the developer, it seems like the list is unbounded. In reality, as the list grows, the data structure may allocate a larger (typically twice the current size) array, copy all its elements to the larger one, and then use that as the underlying array.

In this chapter, we'll look at some common interview questions involving arrays and strategies for solving them. Let's get started!

1.1 Get product of all other elements

Given an array of integers, return a new array such that each element at index i of the new array is the product of all the numbers in the original array except the one at i.

For example, if our input was `[1, 2, 3, 4, 5]`, the expected output would be `[120, 60, 40, 30, 24]`. If our input was `[3, 2, 1]`, the expected output would be `[2, 3, 6]`.

Follow-up: What if you can't use division?

Solution

This problem would be easy with division: an optimal solution could just find the product of all numbers in the array and then divide by each of the numbers. To solve this without division, we will rely on a common technique in array problems: precomputing results from subarrays, and building up a solution from these results.

First note that to find the value associated with the ith element, we must compute the product of all numbers before i and the product of all numbers after i. If we could efficiently calculate these two, we could then simply multiply them to get our desired product.

In order to find the product of numbers before i, we can generate a list of prefix products. Specifically, the ith element in the list will be a product of all numbers including i. Similarly, we can generate a list of suffix products. Finally, for each index we can multiply the appropriate prefix and suffix values to obtain our solution.

```python
def products(nums):
    # Generate prefix products.
    prefix_products = []
    for num in nums:
        if prefix_products:
            prefix_products.append(prefix_products[-1] * num)
        else:
            prefix_products.append(num)

    # Generate suffix products.
    suffix_products = []
    for num in reversed(nums):
        if suffix_products:
            suffix_products.append(suffix_products[-1] * num)
        else:
            suffix_products.append(num)
    suffix_products = list(reversed(suffix_products))

    # Generate result from the product of prefixes and suffixes.
    result = []
    for i in range(len(nums)):
        if i == 0:
```

```
                    result.append(suffix_products[i + 1])
            elif i == len(nums) - 1:
                result.append(prefix_products[i - 1])
            else:
                result.append(
                    prefix_products[i - 1] * suffix_products[i + 1]
                )
        return result
```

This runs in $\mathcal{O}(n)$ time and space, since iterating over the input array takes $\mathcal{O}(n)$ time and the prefix and suffix arrays take up $\mathcal{O}(n)$ space.

1.2 Locate smallest window to be sorted

Given an array of integers that are out of order, determine the bounds of the smallest window that must be sorted in order for the entire array to be sorted. For example, given [3, 7, 5, 6, 9], you should return (1, 3).

Solution

One method we can try is to first find out what the array elements would look like when sorted. For example, [3, 7, 5, 6, 9], after sorting, becomes [3, 5, 6, 7, 9]. We can see that the first and last elements remain unchanged, whereas the middle elements are altered. Therefore, it suffices to take the first and last altered elements as our window.

```
def window(array):
    left, right = None, None
    s = sorted(array)

    for i in range(len(array)):
        if array[i] != s[i] and left is None:
            left = i
        elif array[i] != s[i]:
            right = i
```

```
        return left, right
```

This solution takes $\mathcal{O}(n \log n)$ time and space, since we create a sorted copy of the original array.

Often when dealing with arrays, a more efficient algorithm can be found by looping through the elements and computing a running minimum, maximum, or count. Let's see how we can apply this here.

Suppose instead that we traversed the array, from left to right, and took note of whether each element was less than the maximum seen up to that point. This element would have to be part of the sorting window, since we would have to move the maximum element past it.

As a result, we can take the last element that is less than the running maximum, and use it as our right bound. Similarly, for our left bound, we can traverse the array from right to left, and find the last element that exceeds the running minimum.

This will take two passes over the array, operating in $\mathcal{O}(n)$ time and $\mathcal{O}(1)$ space.

```python
def window(array):
    left, right = None, None
    n = len(array)
    max_seen, min_seen = -float("inf"), float("inf")

    for i in range(n):
        max_seen = max(max_seen, array[i])
        if array[i] < max_seen:
            right = i

    for i in range(n - 1, -1, -1):
        min_seen = min(min_seen, array[i])
        if array[i] > min_seen:
            left = i

    return left, right
```

1.3 Calculate maximum subarray sum

Given an array of numbers, find the maximum sum of any contiguous subarray of the array. For example, given the array [34, -50, 42, 14, -5, 86], the maximum sum would be 137, since we would take elements 42, 14, −5, and 86. Given the array [-5, -1, -8, -9], the maximum sum would be 0, since we would choose not to take any elements.

Do this in $\mathcal{O}(n)$ time.

Follow-up: What if the elements can wrap around? For example, given [8, -1, 3, 4], return 15, as we choose the numbers 3, 4, and 8 where the 8 is obtained from wrapping around.

Solution

The brute force approach here would be to iterate over every contiguous subarray and calculate its sum, keeping track of the largest one seen.

```python
def max_subarray_sum(arr):
    current_max = 0
    for i in range(len(arr) - 1):
        for j in range(i, len(arr)):
            current_max = max(current_max, sum(arr[i:j]))
    return current_max
```

This would run in $\mathcal{O}(n^3)$ time. How can we make this faster?

We can work backwards from our desired solution by iterating over the array and looking at the maximum possible subarray that can be made ending at each index. For each index, we can either include the corresponding element in our sum or exclude it.

As we iterate over our array, we can keep track of the maximum subarray we've seen so far in a variable called `max_so_far`. Whenever we find a larger subarray ending at a given index, we update this variable.

```
def max_subarray_sum(arr):
    max_ending_here = max_so_far = 0
    for x in arr:
        max_ending_here = max(x, max_ending_here + x)
        max_so_far = max(max_so_far, max_ending_here)
    return max_so_far
```

This algorithm is known as Kadane's algorithm, and it runs in $\mathcal{O}(n)$ time and $\mathcal{O}(1)$ space.

We split the follow-up problem into two parts. The first part is the same as before: finding the maximum subarray sum that doesn't wrap around. Next, we compute the maximum subarray sum that **does** wrap around, and take the maximum of the two.

To get the largest wrap-around sum, we can use a little trick. For any subarray that wraps around, there must be some contiguous elements that are excluded, and these elements actually form the minimum possible subarray! Therefore, we can first find the minimum subarray sum using exactly the method above, and subtract this from the array's total.

For example, in the example above, the minimum subarray is [-1], with a total of -1. We then subtract this from the array total, 14, to get 15.

```
def maximum_circular_subarray(arr):
    max_subarray_sum_wraparound = sum(arr) - min_subarray_sum(arr)

    return max(max_subarray_sum(arr), max_subarray_sum_wraparound)

def max_subarray_sum(arr):
    max_ending_here = max_so_far = 0

    for x in arr:
        max_ending_here = max(x, max_ending_here + x)
        max_so_far = max(max_so_far, max_ending_here)

    return max_so_far
```

```
def min_subarray_sum(arr):
    min_ending_here = min_so_far = 0

    for x in arr:
        min_ending_here = min(x, min_ending_here + x)
        min_so_far = min(min_so_far, min_ending_here)

    return min_so_far
```

This takes $\mathcal{O}(n)$ time and $\mathcal{O}(1)$ space.

1.4 Find number of smaller elements to the right

Given an array of integers, return a new array where each element in the new array is the number of smaller elements to the right of that element in the original input array.

For example, given the array [3, 4, 9, 6, 1], return [1, 1, 2, 1, 0], since:

- There is 1 smaller element to the right of 3
- There is 1 smaller element to the right of 4
- There are 2 smaller elements to the right of 9
- There is 1 smaller element to the right of 6
- There are no smaller elements to the right of 1

Solution

A naive solution for this problem would simply be to create a new array, and for each element count all the smaller elements to the right of it.

CHAPTER 1. ARRAYS

```
def smaller_counts_naive(lst):
    result = []
    for i, num in enumerate(lst):
        count = sum(val < num for val in lst[i + 1:])
        result.append(count)
    return result
```

This takes $\mathcal{O}(n^2)$ time. Can we do this any faster?

To speed this up, we can try the following idea:

- Iterate backwards over the input list
- Maintain a sorted list seen of the elements we've seen so far
- Look at seen to see where the current element would fit in

The index will be how many elements on the right are smaller.

```
import bisect

def smaller_counts(lst):
    result = []
    seen = []

    for num in reversed(lst):
        i = bisect.bisect_left(seen, num)
        result.append(i)
        bisect.insort(seen, num)

    return list(reversed(result))
```

Now this only takes $\mathcal{O}(n \log n)$ time and $\mathcal{O}(n)$ space.

Strings

Strings are an unavoidable part of programming. Every word in this sentence, and this whole book itself, can be considered a string! As a result there's a good chance you'll be asked a question involving strings in an interview question.

Behind the scenes, the contents of a string are typically stored in a read-only sequential array in memory, meaning that strings are immutable. In other words, you can reassign a string variable to a new value, but you cannot change a particular character in the underlying array.

The most common operations performed on strings are **indexing** to get a particular character or substring, **joining** two strings together by concatenation, and **splitting** by a delimiter.

Expect to be asked about string rotations, reversals, prefixes and suffixes, and sorting. We'll explore these topics in the following questions.

2.1 Find anagram indices

Given a word w and a string s, find all indices in s which are the starting locations of anagrams of w. For example, given w is ab and s is abxaba, return [0, 3, 4].

Solution

The brute force solution here would be to go over each word-sized window in *s* and check if it forms an anagram, like so:

```python
from collections import Counter

def is_anagram(s1, s2):
    return Counter(s1) == Counter(s2)

def anagram_indices(word, s):
    result = []
    for i in range(len(s) - len(word) + 1):
        window = s[i:i + len(word)]
        if is_anagram(window, word):
            result.append(i)
    return result
```

In the above code, we use Python's built-in `Counter` collection, which when applied to a word forms a dictionary whose keys are characters and whose values are their respective counts.

This would take $\mathcal{O}(w \times s)$ time, where `w` is the length of the word and `s` is the length of the input string. Can we make this any faster?

When approaching any string question, using a hash table should be at the tip of your fingers as a potential strategy. Notice that at each window we are recomputing the frequency counts of the entire window, when only a small part of it actually is updated. If we could efficiently update these frequency counts for each substring, our algorithm would be much quicker.

This insight leads us to the following strategy. First, we make a frequency dictionary of both the initial window and the target word. As we move along the string, we increment the count of each new character and decrement the count of the old. If at any point there is no difference between the frequencies of the target word and the current window, we add the corresponding starting index to our result.

```python
from collections import defaultdict

def del_if_zero(dict, char):
    if dict[char] == 0:
        del dict[char]

def anagram_indices(word, s):
    result = []

    freq = defaultdict(int)
    for char in word:
        freq[char] += 1

    for char in s[:len(word)]:
        freq[char] -= 1
        del_if_zero(freq, char)

    if not freq:
        result.append(0)

    for i in range(len(word), len(s)):
        start_char, end_char = s[i - len(word)], s[i]
        freq[start_char] += 1
        del_if_zero(freq, start_char)

        freq[end_char] -= 1
        del_if_zero(freq, end_char)

        if not freq:
            beginning_index = i - len(word) + 1
            result.append(beginning_index)

    return result
```

This runs in $\mathcal{O}(s)$ time and space.

2.2 Generate palindrome pairs

Given a list of words, find all pairs of unique indices such that the concatenation of the two words is a palindrome.

For example, given the list `["code", "edoc", "da", "d"]`, return `[(0, 1), (1, 0), (2, 3)]`.

Solution

Here we see an example where taking a closer took at substrings yields a significant improvement in efficiency.

One algorithm we can try is to check each possible word pair for palindromicity and add their indices to the result:

```python
def is_palindrome(word):
    return word == word[::-1]

def palindrome_pairs(words):
    result = []

    for i, word1 in enumerate(words):
        for j, word2 in enumerate(words):
            if i == j:
                continue
            if is_palindrome(word1 + word2):
                result.append((i, j))

    return result
```

This takes $\mathcal{O}(n^2 \times c)$ time, where n is the number of words and c is the length of the longest word.

To speed this up, we can insert all words into a dictionary and then check the dictionary for each word's prefixes and suffixes.

Our dictionary will map each word to its index in the list. If the reverse of a word's prefix/suffix is in the dictionary and its corresponding suffix/prefix is palindromic, we add it to our list of results. For example, say we're looking at the word aabc. We check the following prefixes:

- Since "" is a palindrome, we look for cbaa in the dictionary. If we find it, then we can make cbaaaabc.

- Since a is a palindrome, we look for cba in the dictionary. If we find it, then we can make cbaaabc.

- Since aa is a palindrome, we look for cb in the dictionary. If we find it, then we can make cbaabc.

- Since aab and aabc are not palindromes, we don't do anything.

We do the same thing for the suffixes.

```python
def is_palindrome(word):
    return word == word[::-1]

def palindrome_pairs(words):
    d = {}
    for i, word in enumerate(words):
        d[word] = i

    result = []

    for i, word in enumerate(words):
        for char_i in range(len(word)):
            prefix, suffix = word[:char_i], word[char_i:]
            reversed_prefix = prefix[::-1]
            reversed_suffix = suffix[::-1]

            if (is_palindrome(suffix) and
                    reversed_prefix in d):
                if i != d[reversed_prefix]:
                    result.append((i, d[reversed_prefix]))
```

```
            if (is_palindrome(prefix) and
                    reversed_suffix in d):
                if i != d[reversed_suffix]:
                    result.append((d[reversed_suffix], i))

    return result
```

This changes the time complexity to $\mathcal{O}(n \times c^2)$. Since we will likely be constrained more by the number of words than the number of characters, this seems like a significant improvement.

2.3 Print zigzag form

Given a string and a number of lines k, print the string in zigzag form. In zigzag, characters are printed out diagonally from top left to bottom right until reaching the kth line, then back up to top right, and so on.

For example, given the sentence "thisisazigzag" and k = 4, you should print:

```
t     a     g
 h   s z   a
  i i   i z
   s     g
```

Solution

One of the most natural things to do with a string is to print it, so you should be prepared for questions that ask you to print strings in odd ways, such as this one.

One way to solve this would be to go one line at a time, figuring out what that line should be, and printing it. An advantage of this method would be that we would only need $\mathcal{O}(n)$ space at any given time, where n is the length of a line. Let's see how this would work.

CHAPTER 2. STRINGS

For the zigzag pattern above, we can see that the letters in the top and bottom lines are each separated by 5 spaces. What about the middle lines? Here it is trickier — it depends on whether the pattern is descending or ascending. When we are ascending, we should put 3 spaces after the second line and 1 space after the third line, but if we are ascending the reverse is true.

Let's try to clear up this confusion by looking at what happens with 5 lines:

```
t       o       z
 h     n t     g a
  i   a   h   i   g
   s s     e z
    i       r
```

Here as we move from top to bottom there are 7, 5, 3, and 1 spaces added after each letter, and the same is true when we go from bottom to top.

So if `row` is the current row we're on, `desc` represents whether or not we are descending, and `k` is the number of lines, we can predict the number of tacked-on spaces using the following formula:

```
def get_spaces(row, desc, k):
    max_spaces = (k - 1) * 2 - 1
    if desc:
        spaces = max_spaces - row * 2
    else:
        spaces = max_spaces - (k - 1 - row) * 2
    return spaces
```

This presents us with another challenge: how do we know whether or not the pattern is descending? Note that if we have five rows, we will be descending for the first four, ascending for the next four, and so on. This can be represented mathematically like so:

```
def is_descending(index, k):
    # Check whether the index is more or less than halfway
```

```
        # through its oscillation back to the starting point.
        return index % (2 * (k - 1)) < k - 1
```

Putting these together, our algorithm will create a list of empty strings for the first row. After placing the first character in this list at the appropriate index, it will check whether the pattern is ascending or descending, find out how many spaces are needed, and move to the next index. When we get to the end of the row, we print it out, and repeat this process for subsequent rows.

```
def zigzag(sentence, k):
    n = len(sentence)

    for row in range(k):
        i = row
        line = [" " for _ in range(n)]

        while i < n:
            line[i] = sentence[i]
            desc = is_descending(i, k)
            spaces = get_spaces(row, desc, k)
            i += spaces + 1

        print("".join(line))
```

Even though `is_descending` and `get_spaces` are constant-time operations, we still need to join and print each line of the string, which will take $\mathcal{O}(n)$ time, so the whole algorithm will be $\mathcal{O}(k \times n)$.

2.4 Determine smallest rotated string

You are given a string of length n and an integer k. The string can be manipulated by taking one of the first k letters and moving it to the end of the string.

Write a program to determine the lexicographically smallest string that can be created after an unlimited number of moves.

CHAPTER 2. STRINGS

For example, suppose we are given the string `daily` and $k = 1$. The best we can create in this case is `ailyd`.

Solution

Sorting strings is something we will revisit in the chapter on sorting, but this question gives us a glimpse into the type of operations that are helpful.

We can break this problem down into two cases.

First, consider the case where $k = 1$. Here we are only allowed to rotate the string, so we can simply choose the alphabetically earliest rotation.

Now suppose $k > 1$. This situation is a bit trickier, as it seems we must figure out which of the first k items to move at each step. However, it turns out that there is a series of moves that allows us to effectively swap any two letters.

We can understand these moves by looking at the general example of converting xxabxx to xxbaxx. In the table below, each string represents the newly formed result of the preceding transformation.

String	Transformation
xxabxx	Move all x to end, one at a time
abxxxx	Move b to end
axxxxb	Move a to end
xxxxba	Move x to end, one at a time, until reaching initial position
xxbaxx	Swapped

In code, this would look like the following:

```python
def bubble_swap(string, i, j):
    string = list(string)

    # Rotate so that i is at the beginning.
    while i > 0:
        string = string[1:] + string[:1]
```

```
        i -= 1

    # Move the first two letters to the end in reversed order.
    string = string[:1] + string[2:] + string[1:2]
    string = string[1:] + string[:1]

    # Rotate back to the initial position.
    while len(string) > j + 1:
        string = string[1:] + string[:1]
        j += 1

    return ''.join(string)
```

As indicated by the name, this operation is essentially the same as that used for bubble sort. Therefore, so long as we are allowed to move either the first or second letter, we can always obtain a fully sorted string.

Our full solution, then, will be to return the alphabetically earliest rotation if $k = 1$, and otherwise the sorted string.

```
def get_best_word(string, k):
    string = list(string)

    if k == 1:
        best = string
        for i in range(1, len(string)):
            if string[i:] + string[:i] < best:
                best = string[i:] + string[:i]
        return ''.join(best)

    else:
        return ''.join(sorted(string))
```

In the first case, our algorithm loops through n rotations and compares two strings of length n, for a time complexity of $\mathcal{O}(n^2)$. The space required will be $\mathcal{O}(n)$, the size of our two string variables.

For the latter, sorting our string will take $\mathcal{O}(n \log n)$ time, and building the new string will require $\mathcal{O}(n)$ space.

3

Linked Lists

One way you can think of a linked list is as a music playlist, where each item contains the song to be played and a "next song" button. In this abstract playlist, you cannot play any song you want; to play a given song you must play through all the songs before it first.

There are two main kinds of linked lists. Singly linked lists only contain a pointer to the next node, typically called `next`, and are implemented as follows:

```python
class Node:
    def __init__(self, data, next=None):
        self.data = data
        self.next = next
```

Linked lists are a recursive data structure: the type of `next` is another linked list node. Because of this, linked lists have no fixed size like arrays do: a new node can be initialized and appended to a linked list on the fly.

Doubly linked lists, meanwhile, have pointers to the previous and next nodes. They take up more space, but allow you to traverse backwards. The implementation for a doubly linked list looks like this:

```python
class Node:
    def __init__(self, data, next=None, prev=None):
        self.data = data
        self.next = next
        self.prev = prev
```

Returning to the analogy above, a doubly linked list would mean that each song has both a "previous song" and "next song" button.

Common operations on linked lists include searching, appending, prepending, and removing nodes. You should be able to quickly write an implementation of each of these in an interview.

In an interview setting, you should be prepared to answer questions about traversing and reversing linked lists, as well as rearranging their nodes. Let's try out a few problems!

3.1 Reverse linked list

Given the head of a singly linked list, reverse it in-place.

Solution

Reversing a linked list is a classic interview question that can be surprisingly tricky if you've never tried it before, so this problem merits close attention.

First, let's consider a few cases. What if the linked list has just one element, such as 15? Then we only need to return that node, since it is already sorted. Now how about if the linked list has two elements? Here, we need to rearrange the pointers so that the tail becomes the head, and the head becomes the tail.

To solve this problem more generally, we must think recursively. We will explain recursion more fully in a later chapter, but since the concept pops up frequently in linked list questions it will be useful to work through an example here.

CHAPTER 3. LINKED LISTS

For any recursive solution we require a base case and an inductive case. What are the base cases here? For an empty linked list, we should return null, since it is trivially already sorted. Similarly, for a linked list with one element, we need only return that one element.

Now let's consider a linked list with an arbitrary number of elements. How can we reverse it, assuming we can reverse smaller linked lists in place? Suppose we take the head node and store it in a variable somewhere. Then, we can take the head's next, which is a smaller linked list, and recursively reverse that — let's call this smaller, reverse linked list s. Finally, the head must be reattached to the end of s, after which we return the head of s.

Let s be the tail of the linked list (the list without the head):

Recursively call reverse on the tail, and then reattach a to the end:

Note that we have created a helper function to return both the head and the tail of the linked list, to simplify our logic.

```
def reverse(node):
    # _reverse() reverses and returns both head and tail.
    # Conventionally, an underscore denotes an unused variable.
    head, _ = _reverse(node)
    return head

def _reverse(node):
    if node is None:
        return None, None

    if node.next is None:
        return node, node

    # Reverse rest of linked list and move node to after tail.
```

```
        head, tail = _reverse(node.next)
        node.next = None
        tail.next = node
        return head, node
```

This runs in $\mathcal{O}(n)$ time, which is optimal — we cannot reverse a list without traversing through all its elements at least once. However, it also runs in $\mathcal{O}(n)$ space, since each call to reverse adds to our call stack.

Ideally, what we would like to do is update the list as we traverse it. As we do so, we will need to change each node so that it points to the node that came before it, instead of the one after. To help us implement this, we will use a technique that is very common in linked list problems: iterating over the list with two pointers.

In particular, we will maintain two pointers, current and prev. As the current pointer traverses the list, prev follows one node behind. At each step, we will set the current node's next to point to the previous node, and then move both pointers forward. Finally, we return the last node.

```
def reverse(head):
    prev, current = None, head
    while current is not None:
        # Make current node point to prev and move both forward one.
        tmp = current.next
        current.next = prev
        prev = current
        current = tmp
    return prev
```

Our new and improved solution now only uses constant space!

3.2 Add two linked lists that represent numbers

We can represent an integer in a linked list format by having each node represent a digit in the number. The nodes are connected in reverse order, such that the number

CHAPTER 3. LINKED LISTS   45

54321 is represented by the following linked list:

Given two linked lists in this format, return their sum.

For example, given:

You should return 124 (99 + 25) as:

Solution

In a problem such as this one, knowing how to iterate through a linked list gets you halfway to a solution. More concretely, we can add two numbers using the same process as elementary grade school addition: adding the least significant digits with a carry.

We'll start at the head of the two nodes, and compute the sum of both values modulo 10. We write this down, move the two nodes up and add a carry if the sum was greater than 10. A tricky part here is finding the terminating condition. We can see that this happens when there is no more carry and the two linked lists have reached the end. Once this happens, we extend the nodes one more until they are both None and carry is 0 and then return None.

```
def add(node0, node1, carry=0):
    if not node0 and not node1 and not carry:
```

```
            return None

    node0_val = node0.data if node0 else 0
    node1_val = node1.data if node1 else 0
    total = node0_val + node1_val + carry

    node0_next = node0.next if node0 else None
    node1_next = node1.next if node1 else None
    carry_next = 1 if total >= 10 else 0

    return Node(total % 10, add(node0_next, node1_next, carry_next))
```

This will run in $\mathcal{O}(m + n)$ time, where m and n are the lengths of the two linked lists.

3.3 Rearrange a linked list to alternate high-low

Given a linked list, rearrange the node values such that they appear in alternating low → high → low → high → ... form.

For example, given $1 \to 2 \to 3 \to 4 \to 5$, you should return $1 \to 3 \to 2 \to 5 \to 4$.

Solution

Let's take a look at the example input and see if we can derive an algorithm. One straightforward method is to examine each consecutive pair of nodes, and perform a swap if they do not alternate as required. For the example above, we would carry out the following steps:

- 1 < 2? Yes, proceed with $1 \to 2$

- 2 > 3? No, swap these values to end up with $1 \to 3 \to 2$

- 2 < 4? Yes, proceed with $1 \to 3 \to 2 \to 4$

- 4 > 5? No, swap these values to end up with $1 \to 3 \to 2 \to 5 \to 4$

CHAPTER 3. LINKED LISTS

In order to implement this, we must know at any given time whether a node's value should be less than or greater than that of its successor. To do this we can use a variable that is True at even nodes, and False at odd ones.

```
def alternate(ll):
    even = True
    cur = ll

    while cur.next:
        if cur.data > cur.next.data and even:
            cur.data, cur.next.data = cur.next.data, cur.data

        elif cur.data < cur.next.data and not even:
            cur.data, cur.next.data = cur.next.data, cur.data

        even = not even
        cur = cur.next

    return ll
```

While this works, the use of even is somewhat inelegant. Note that in order for the node values to alternate in this way, it must be true that every odd node's value is greater than its preceding and succeeding values. So an alternative algorithm would be to check every other node, and perform the following swaps:

- If the previous node's value is greater, swap the current and previous values.

- If the next node's value is greater, swap the current and next values.

Instead of using a variable for parity, we can use two pointers that jump forward two steps after each check.

```
def alternate(ll):
    prev = ll
    cur = ll.next
```

```
        while cur:
            if prev.data > cur.data:
                prev.data, cur.data = cur.data, prev.data

            if not cur.next:
                break

            if cur.next.data > cur.data:
                cur.next.data, cur.data = cur.data, cur.next.data

            prev = cur.next
            cur = cur.next.next

    return ll
```

Both of these algorithms use $\mathcal{O}(n)$ time and $\mathcal{O}(1)$ space, since we must traverse the entire linked list, and we are only tracking one or two nodes at a time.

3.4 Find intersecting nodes of linked lists

Given two singly linked lists that intersect at some point, find the intersecting node. Assume the lists are non-cyclical.

For example, given $A = 3 \to 7 \to 8 \to 10$ and $B = 99 \to 1 \to 8 \to 10$, return the node with value 8. In this example, assume nodes with the same value are the exact same node objects.

Do this in $\mathcal{O}(m + n)$ time (where m and n are the lengths of the lists) and constant space.

Solution

To handle this problem, we will again use our favorite linked list tactic: iterating with two pointers. Let's start by first ignoring the time and space constraints, in order to get a better grasp of the problem.

CHAPTER 3. LINKED LISTS

Naively, we could iterate through one of the lists and add each node to a set. Then we could iterate over the other list and check each node to see if it is in the set, and return the first node present in the set. This takes $\mathcal{O}(m+n)$ time and also $\mathcal{O}(m+n)$ space (since we don't know initially which list is longer). How can we reduce the amount of space we need?

We can get around the space constraint with the following trick: first, get the length of both lists. Find the difference between the two, and then keep two pointers at the head of each list. Move the pointer of the larger list up by the difference, and then move the pointers forward in conjunction until they match.

```python
def length(head):
    if not head:
        return 0
    return 1 + length(head.next)

def intersection(a, b):
    m, n = length(a), length(b)
    cur_a, cur_b = a, b

    if m > n:
        for _ in range(m - n):
            cur_a = cur_a.next
    else:
        for _ in range(n - m):
            cur_b = cur_b.next

    while cur_a != cur_b:
        cur_a = cur_a.next
        cur_b = cur_b.next
    return cur_a
```

4

Stacks and Queues

When you find yourself needing to frequently add and remove items from a list, stacks and queues are two data structures that you should consider.

To understand how a stack works, imagine a literal stack of cafeteria trays. Adding a new one to the top, and removing the top one can be done quickly, whereas it is difficult (read: not allowed) to change trays from the middle. This property is known by the shorthand "last in, first out", or **LIFO**.

The traditional names for these operations, as well as a method for checking the value of the top "tray", are given in the following implementation, in which all methods are $\mathcal{O}(1)$:

```python
class Stack:
    def __init__(self):
        self.stack = []

    def push(self, x):
        # Add an item to the stack.
        self.stack.append(x)

    def pop(self):
        # Remove and return the top element.
        return self.stack.pop()
```

```
    def peek(self):
        return self.stack[-1]
```

Note that a pop operation on an empty stack will result in an exception, unless there is proper error handling.

In the above implementation we have used a Python list as the underlying data structure, meaning the size of the stack will dynamically resize as necessary. Alternatively we could have used a linked list, so that new elements would be added to, and removed from, the tail of the existing chain.

A queue, on the other hand, can be thought of as a group of people standing in line, perhaps waiting to buy this book. Each person enters the line from the back, and leaves in exactly the order that they entered it, a property known as "first in, first out", or **FIFO**.

Queues are commonly implemented as linked lists, where we enqueue and item by adding a tail node and dequeue an item by removing the head node and moving our head pointer forward.

In a double-ended queue, one can efficiently append and remove items to either side of the list. Python provides the built-in collections.deque library for this purpose, which uses the following API:

```
from collections import deque

queue = deque()

queue.append(4)
queue.append(5)
queue.appendleft(6)

print(queue) # deque([6, 4, 5])

queue.popleft() # 6
queue.pop() # 5
```

```
    print(queue) # deque([4])
```

The append and popleft operations above are more traditionally called enqueue and dequeue, so in the following questions we will frequently use the latter terminology. Along with pop and appendleft, these operations run in $\mathcal{O}(1)$ time.

When the most recent item examined is the most important, a stack is frequently a good choice. For this reason stacks often feature in depth-first search, backtracking, and syntax parsing applications.

When the order of the items you are dealing with needs to be preserved, on the other hand, a queue is preferable. Queues can be found, for example, in breadth-first search, buffers, and scheduling applications.

4.1 Implement a max stack

Implement a stack that has the following methods:

- push(val): push val onto the stack

- pop: pop off and return the topmost element of the stack. If there are no elements in the stack, throw an error.

- max: return the maximum value in the stack currently. If there are no elements in the stack, throw an error.

Each method should run in constant time.

Solution

Implementing the stack part (push and pop) of this problem is easy — we can just use a typical list to implement the stack with append and pop. However, getting the max in constant time is a little trickier. We could do this in linear time if we popped off everything on the stack while keeping track of the maximum value, and then put everything back on.

To accomplish this in constant time, we can use a secondary stack that **only** keeps track of the max values at any time. It will have the exact same number of elements as our primary stack at any point in time, but the top of the stack will always contain the maximum value of the stack.

We can then, when pushing, check if the element we're pushing is greater than the max value of the secondary stack (by just looking at the top), and if it is, then push that instead. If not, we append the previous value.

```python
class MaxStack:
    def __init__(self):
        self.stack = []
        self.maxes = []

    def push(self, val):
        self.stack.append(val)
        if self.maxes:
            self.maxes.append(max(val, self.maxes[-1]))
        else:
            self.maxes.append(val)

    def pop(self):
        if self.maxes:
            self.maxes.pop()
        return self.stack.pop()

    def max(self):
        return self.maxes[-1]
```

4.2 Determine whether brackets are balanced

Given a string of round, curly, and square opening and closing brackets, return whether the brackets are balanced (well-formed).

CHAPTER 4. STACKS AND QUEUES

For example, given the string `"([])[]({})"`, you should return true.

Given the string `"([)]"` or `"((()"`, you should return false.

Solution

Let's start with a simplified case of the problem: dealing with only round brackets. Notice that in this case, we only need to keep track of the current number of opening brackets — each closing bracket should be matched with the rightmost opening bracket. So we can keep a counter and increment it for every opening bracket we see and decrement it on every closing bracket. If we get to the end of the string and our counter is non-zero, our brackets will be unbalanced. A negative number would indicate more closing brackets than opening ones, and a positive number would indicate the opposite.

In the case of round, curly, and square brackets, we need to also keep track of what **kind** of brackets they are, because we can't match a round opening bracket with a curly or square closing bracket. A stack is an ideal data structure for this type of problem, since it can keep track of which depth level we're at. We'll use a stack to keep track of the actual characters. We push onto it when we encounter an opening bracket, and pop whenever we encounter a matching closing bracket. If the stack is empty or it's not the correct matching bracket, then we will return `False`. If at the end of the iteration we have something left over in the stack, our input is sure to be unbalanced. As a result we can return a boolean value representing whether or not our stack is empty.

```python
def balance(s):
    stack = []
    for char in s:
        if char in ["(", "[", "{"]:
            stack.append(char)
        else:
            # Check character is not unmatched
            if not stack:
                return False

            # Char is a closing bracket. Check top of stack if it
```

```
            # matches
            if (char == ")" and stack[-1] != "(" or \
                (char == "]" and stack[-1] != "[" or \
                (char == "}" and stack[-1] != "{"):
                    return False
            stack.pop()

    return len(stack) == 0
```

This takes $\mathcal{O}(n)$ time and space, where n is the number of characters in s.

Fun fact: "(())" is not a palindrome, nor is "()()". "())(" is a palindrome, though.

4.3 Compute maximum of k-length subarrays

Given an array of integers and a number k, where $1 \leq k \leq$ array length, compute the maximum values of each subarray of length k.

For example, let's say the array is `[10, 5, 2, 7, 8, 7]` and $k = 3$. We should get `[10, 7, 8, 8]`, since:

- 10 = max(10, 5, 2)
- 7 = max(5, 2, 7)
- 8 = max(2, 7, 8)
- 8 = max(7, 8, 7)

Do this in $\mathcal{O}(n)$ time and $\mathcal{O}(k)$ space. You can modify the input array in-place and you do not need to store the results. You can simply print them out as you compute them.

CHAPTER 4. STACKS AND QUEUES

Solution

Let's first write out a naive solution: we can simply take each subarray of length k and compute its maximum.

```python
def max_of_subarrays(lst, k):
    for i in range(len(lst) - k + 1):
        print(max(lst[i:i + k]))
```

This takes $\mathcal{O}(n \times k)$ time, which doesn't quite get us to where we want. How can we make this faster?

Notice that, for example, for the input [1, 2, 3, 4, 5, 6, 7, 8, 9] and k = 3, after evaluating the max of the first range, since 3 is at the end, we only need to check whether 4 is greater than 3. If it is, then we can print 4 immediately, and if it isn't, we can stick with 3.

On the other hand, for the input [9, 8, 7, 6, 5, 4, 3, 2, 1] and $k = 3$, after evaluating the max of the first range, we can't do the same thing, since we can't use 9 again. We have to look at 8 instead, and then once we move on to the next range, we have to look at 7.

These two data points suggest an idea: we can keep a double-ended queue with max size k and only keep what we need to evaluate in it. That is, if we see [1, 3, 5], then we only need to keep [5], since we know that 1 and 3 cannot possibly be the maxes.

So what we can do is maintain an ordered list of indices, where we only keep the elements we care about. That is, we will maintain the loop invariant that our queue is always ordered so that we only keep the maximal indices.

It will help to go over an example. Consider our test input: [10, 5, 2, 7, 8, 7] and $k = 3$. Our queue at each step would look like this (recall that these are really indices):

First, we preprocess the first k elements to get our window to size k:

Process 10. We add it to the queue.

$$\boxed{10}$$

Process 5. 5 is smaller than 10, so we keep 10 at the front.

$$\boxed{10\ |\ 5}$$

Process 2. 2 is smaller than 5, so we keep 10 and 5 in the list.

$$\boxed{10\ |\ 5\ |\ 2}$$

Then we begin our main loop:

Print first element in queue and dequeue it: 10

Process 7. 7 is bigger than 2 and 5, so we pop them off.

$$\boxed{7}$$

Print first element in queue and dequeue: 7

Process 8.

$$\boxed{8}$$

Print first element in queue and dequeue: 8

7 is smaller than 8, so we keep 8 in the queue.

CHAPTER 4. STACKS AND QUEUES

| 8 | 7 |

Print first element in queue and dequeue: 8

Done!

Here is how we could implement this in Python.

```python
from collections import deque

def max_of_subarrays(lst, k):
    q = deque()
    for i in range(k):
        while q and lst[i] >= lst[q[-1]]:
            q.pop()
        q.append(i)

    # Loop invariant: q is a list of indices where their
    # corresponding values are in descending order.
    for i in range(k, len(lst)):
        print(lst[q[0]])
        while q and q[0] <= i - k:
            q.popleft()
        while q and lst[i] >= lst[q[-1]]:
            q.pop()
        q.append(i)
    print(lst[q[0]])
```

We've now achieved our desired $\mathcal{O}(n)$ time and $\mathcal{O}(k)$ space!

4.4 Reconstruct array using +/- signs

The sequence [0, 1, ..., N] has been jumbled, and the only clue you have for its order is an array representing whether each number is larger or smaller than the last. Given this information, reconstruct an array that is consistent with it. For example, given [None, +, +, -, +], you could return [1, 2, 3, 0, 4].

Solution

Notice that if there are no negative signs in our input, we can return the original sequence [0, 1, ..., N]. Furthermore, if we have just one run of consecutive negatives, we can reverse the corresponding entries in the original sequence to produce a decreasing run of numbers. For example, given [None, +, -, -, -] we can reverse the last three entries of [0, 1, 2, 3, 4] to get [0, 1, 4, 3, 2].

We can extend this trick to more complicated input, matching plus signs with elements of our original sequence and reversing subsequences whenever there is a run of minus signs.

To keep track of which numbers are being reversed, we can use a stack. As we traverse the input array, we keep track of the corresponding elements of the original sequence. For a run of positive signs, we keep the elements from the original sequence. For a run of negative signs, we push those elements onto the stack. When the run of negatives ends, we can pop those elements off one by one to get a decreasing subsequence in our answer.

Since there is one fewer + or - sign than elements in our answer, the last element must be generated separately. Additionally, a run of negative signs can end with either a positive or the end of the input array, so we must make sure to empty the stack at the end.

```python
def reconstruct(array):
    answer = []
    n = len(array) - 1
    stack = []

    for i in range(n):
        if array[i + 1] == '-':
            stack.append(i)
        else:
            answer.append(i)
            while stack:
                answer.append(stack.pop())

    stack.append(n)
```

```
    while stack:
        answer.append(stack.pop())

    return answer
```

This algorithm runs in $\mathcal{O}(n)$ time and space, since in the worst case we are filling up a stack the same size as our original array. It may seem as if there is a higher time complexity because of our inner loop over the stack, but the total number of items we pop off is bounded by the size of the input array.

5

Hash Tables

A hash table is a crucial tool to keep in your data structure arsenal. Simply put, hash tables associate keys with values using a hash function, allowing for $\mathcal{O}(1)$ lookup, insert, and delete times.

You may be wondering, what's the catch? For one, not everything can be hashed. It is necessary that keys be immutable, so for example Python lists cannot be used as keys. Additionally, under the hood there may be a lot of work needed to implement a rigorous hash function. However, in an interview setting there aren't too many downsides: if you see an opportunity to use a hash table, use it.

In Python, hash tables are closely tied to dictionaries, and use the following syntax:

```
d = {}

d['key'] = 'value'
print(d['key']) # 'value'

del d['key']
print(d['key']) # KeyError: 'key'

if 'key' in d:
    print(d['key'])
```

```
else:
    print("key doesn't exist")
```

Note from above that if a key does not exist in a dictionary, simply trying to get the value will cause a `KeyError`.

The last few lines show one way of getting around this. In the solutions that follow, we will instead use the `defaultdict` library, which allows you pass in a `callable` parameter when declaring a dictionary to set the default value for each key.

A common motivating example for using hash tables is the two-sum problem, stated as follows:

Given a list of numbers and a number k, return whether any two numbers from the list add up to k. For example, given `[10, 15, 3, 7]` and $k = 17$, we should return `True`, since $10 + 7 = 17$.

Instead of a brute force solution which checks all pairs of integers to search for this total, we can use the following strategy. For each value we come across, we store it in a hash table with the value `True`. We then check if the key `k - value` exists in the table, and if so we can return `True`.

```
def two_sum(lst, k):
    seen = {}
    for num in lst:
        if k - num in seen:
            return True
        seen[num] = True
    return False
```

This implementation cuts our time complexity down from $\mathcal{O}(n^2)$ to $\mathcal{O}(n)$, since each lookup is $\mathcal{O}(1)$.

As the problem above demonstrates, if an interviewer asks you to make a solution more efficient, a dictionary should be the first tool you look for.

Let's now look at some other uses of hash tables.

CHAPTER 5. HASH TABLES

5.1 Implement an LRU cache

Implement an LRU (Least Recently Used) cache. The cache should be able to be initialized with cache size n, and provide the following methods:

- `set(key, value)`: set key to value. If there are already n items in the cache and we are adding a new item, also remove the least recently used item.
- `get(key)`: get the value at key. If no such key exists, return null.

Each operation should run in $\mathcal{O}(1)$ time.

Solution

Hash tables are commonly used as the underlying data structure for a cache. This problem gives us a taste of how this can be done.

To implement both these methods in constant time, we'll need to combine our hash table with a linked list. The hash table will map keys to nodes in the linked list, and the linked list will be ordered from least recently used to most recently used.

The logic behind each functions will be as follows.

For set:

- First look at our current capacity. If it's less than n, create a node with the given value, set it as the head, and add it as an entry in the dictionary.
- If it's equal to n, add our node as usual, but also evict the least frequently used node. We can achieve this by deleting the head of our linked list and removing the entry from our dictionary.

We'll need to keep track of the key in each node so that we know which entry to evict.

For get:

- If the key doesn't exist in our dictionary, return null.

- Otherwise, look up the relevant node in the dictionary. Before returning it, update the linked list by moving the node to the tail of the list.

To keep our logic clean, we will implement a `LinkedList` helper class that allows us to reuse methods when adding and removing nodes. In particular, we will use the add and remove methods of this class when bumping a node to the back of the list after fetching it.

In the end, the code would look like this:

```python
class Node:
    def __init__(self, key, val):
        self.key = key
        self.val = val
        self.prev = None
        self.next = None

class LinkedList:
    def __init__(self):
        # Create dummy nodes and set up head <-> tail.
        self.head = Node(None, 'head')
        self.tail = Node(None, 'tail')

        self.head.next = self.tail
        self.tail.prev = self.head

    def get_head(self):
        return self.head.next

    def get_tail(self):
        return self.tail.prev

    def add(self, node):
        prev = self.tail.prev
        prev.next = node
        node.prev = prev
        node.next = self.tail
        self.tail.prev = node
```

```python
    def remove(self, node):
        prev = node.prev
        nxt = node.next
        prev.next = nxt
        nxt.prev = prev

class LRUCache:
    def __init__(self, n):
        self.n = n
        self.dict = {}
        self.list = LinkedList()

    def set(self, key, val):
        if key in self.dict:
            self.dict[key].delete()

        n = Node(key, val)
        self.list.add(n)
        self.dict[key] = n

        if len(self.dict) > self.n:
            head = self.list.get_head()
            self.list.remove(head)
            del self.dict[head.key]

    def get(self, key):
        if key in self.dict:
            n = self.dict[key]

            # Bump to the back of the list by removing and adding the node.
            self.list.remove(n)
            self.list.add(n)
            return n.val
```

All of these operations run in $\mathcal{O}(1)$ time.

5.2 Cut brick wall

A wall consists of several rows of bricks of various integer lengths and uniform height. Your goal is to find a vertical line going from the top to the bottom of the wall that cuts through the fewest number of bricks. If the line goes through the edge between two bricks, this does not count as a cut.

For example, suppose the input is as follows, where values in each row represent the lengths of bricks in that row:

```
[[3, 5, 1, 1],
 [2, 3, 3, 2],
 [5, 5],
 [4, 4, 2],
 [1, 3, 3, 3],
 [1, 1, 6, 1, 1]]
```

The wall would then look like this:

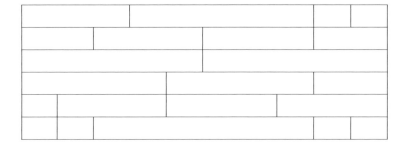

The best we can we do here is to draw a line after the eighth brick, which will only require cutting through the bricks in the third and fifth row.

Given an input consisting of brick lengths for each row such as the one above, return the fewest number of bricks that must be cut to create a vertical line.

Solution

At first glance we might consider testing each vertical line to see how many bricks it would have to cut through. However, given the structure of our input, each line will require us to accumulate the values of each row of bricks, which will be both messy and time-consuming. If the length of the wall is m and there are n total bricks, this will take $\mathcal{O}(m \times n)$.

Let's reframe this with a little help from our friend the hash table. Instead of thinking about how to minimize the number of cuts, we can try to maximize the number of times a line can pass through an edge between two bricks.

To do this, we will examine each row and increment a counter in a hash table for the accumulated distance covered after each brick, except for the last one. For example, after the first row in the input above, our map would contain {3: 1, 8: 1, 9: 1}. The key in the dictionary with the largest value represents the vertical line with the fewest bricks cut. Finally, to find the actual number of bricks, we can subtract this value from the total number of rows.

```
from collections import defaultdict

def fewest_cuts(wall):
    cuts = defaultdict(int)

    for row in wall:
        length = 0
        for brick in row[:-1]:
            length += brick
            cuts[length] += 1

    return len(wall) - max(cuts.values())
```

For each brick, we only need to update our dictionary once, so this algorithm will take $O(n)$ time. Our map will require $O(m)$ space to store a value for each possible edge.

5.3 Implement a sparse array

You have a large array, most of whose elements are zero.

Create a more space-efficient data structure, `SparseArray`, that implements the following interface:

- `init(arr, size)`: initialize with the original large array and size.
- `set(i, val)`: update index at i to be `val`.
- `get(i)`: get the value at index i.

Solution

One advantage hash tables have over other data structures is that data need not be sequential. If we wanted to set the 1000th value in a `1024-bit` array, we still need to store zeroes for all the other bits.

With a hash table, however, we can cut down on space tremendously by only keeping track of the non-zero values and indices. We will use a dictionary that stores only these values and defaults to zero if any key is not found.

We must also remember to check the bounds when setting or getting i, and to clean up any indices if we're setting an index to zero again, to save space.

```python
class SparseArray:
    def __init__(self, arr, n):
        self.n = n
        self._dict = {}
        for i, e in enumerate(arr):
            if e != 0:
                self._dict[i] = e

    def _check_bounds(self, i):
        if i < 0 or i >= self.n:
            raise IndexError('Out of bounds')
```

```python
    def set(self, i, val):
        self._check_bounds(i)
        if val != 0:
            self._dict[i] = val
            return
        elif i in self._dict:
            del self._dict[i]

    def get(self, i):
        self._check_bounds(i)
        return self._dict.get(i, 0)
```

Thanks to the magic of hash tables, our implementation will only use as much space as there are non-zero elements in the array.

6

Trees

Trees are among the most common topics asked about in software interviews. Fortunately, with a few key concepts under your belt you should be well prepared to answer any of these questions.

You probably have an intuitive understanding of trees, as they pop up frequently enough outside of computer science: family tree diagrams, grammar parsing, and flow charts are some contexts in which they may be found. Here we present a slightly more restricted definition: a tree is a recursive data structure consisting of a **root** node (typically shown at the top) with zero or more **child** nodes, where each child node acts as the root of a new tree.

For example, below is a binary tree rooted at 7. Binary here means simply that each node is only allowed to have up to two **leaf** nodes.

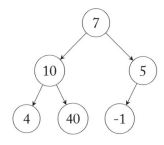

Note that we make no restriction at the moment as to the values of the tree. In the next chapter, we will explore binary search trees, which impose a specific ordering on the values of child and parent nodes.

Trees are **directed** and **acyclic**: the connections between parents and children always flow downward, so that it is impossible to form a loop. Further, in contrast to a typical family tree, two parents can never have the same child.

Common operations in tree questions involve:

- inserting, searching for, and deleting a particular node
- finding subtrees, or a subset of nodes that form their own tree
- determining the distance or relationship between two nodes

Typically to answer these questions you will need to perform a recursive tree traversal, which comes in three flavors:

- in-order: Traverse left node, then current node, then right
- pre-order: Traverse current node, then left node, then right
- post-order: Traverse left node, then right node, then current

For the tree above, for example, the three traversals would generate the following orders, respectively:

- [4, 10, 40, 7, -1, 5]
- [7, 10, 4, 40, 5, -1]
- [4, 40, 10, -1, 5, 7]

In the problems in this chapter we will explore the tradeoffs between these more deeply.

There are a few additional pieces of terminology you should be familiar with when dealing with trees:

CHAPTER 6. TREES

- A node A is called an **ancestor** of a node B if it can be found on the path from the root to B.

- The **height** or **depth** of a tree is the length of the longest path from the root to any leaf.

- A **full** binary tree is a binary tree in which every non-leaf node has exactly two children.

- A **complete** binary tree is one in which all levels except for the bottom one are full, and all nodes on the bottom level are filled in left to right.

To implement a tree, we typically begin by defining a `Node` class and then using it to build a `Tree` class.

```
class Node:
    def __init__(self, data, left=None, right=None):
        self.data = data
        self.left = left
        self.right = right
```

The implementation of a given tree will often depend on the tree's application, and the particular traversal algorithm chosen. For an example, take a look at the binary search tree definition in the following chapter.

As mentioned above, trees can represent a wide variety of objects: animal classification schemas, an HTML document object model, moves in a chess game, or a Linux file system are a few. In general when you are faced with hierarchical data, trees are a great data structure to choose.

6.1 Count unival trees

A unival tree (which stands for "universal value") is a tree where all nodes under it have the same value.

Given the root to a binary tree, count the number of unival subtrees.

CHAPTER 6. TREES

For example, the following tree has 5 unival subtrees:

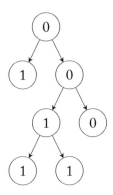

Solution

To start off, we should go through some examples.

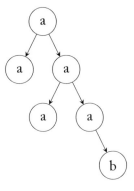

This tree has 3 unival subtrees: the two a leaves, and the one b leaf. The b leaf causes all its parents to not be counted as a unival tree.

CHAPTER 6. TREES

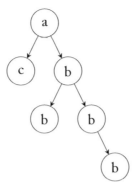

This tree has 5 unival subtrees: the leaf at c, and every b.

Let's begin by first writing a function that checks whether a tree is unival or not. Then, perhaps we could use this to count up all the nodes in the tree.

To check whether a tree is a unival tree, we must check that every node in the tree has the same value. To start off, we could define an is_unival function that takes in a root to a tree. We would do this recursively with a helper function. Recall that a leaf qualifies as a unival tree.

```python
def is_unival(root):
    return unival_helper(root, root.value)

def unival_helper(root, value):
    if root is None:
        return True

    if root.value == value:
        return unival_helper(root.left, value) and \
               unival_helper(root.right, value)

    return False
```

And then our function that counts the number of subtrees could simply use that function:

```python
def count_unival_subtrees(root):
    if root is None:
```

```
        return 0

    left = count_unival_subtrees(root.left)
    right = count_unival_subtrees(root.right)

    return 1 + left + right if is_unival(root) else left + right
```

However, this runs in $\mathcal{O}(n^2)$ time. For each node of the tree, we're evaluating each node in its subtree again as well. We can improve the runtime by starting at the leaves of the tree, and keeping track of the unival subtree count as we percolate back up. In this way we evaluate each node only once, making our algorithm run in $\mathcal{O}(n)$ time.

```
def count_unival_subtrees(root):
    count, _ = helper(root)
    return count

# Return the number of unival subtrees, and a Boolean for
# whether the root is itself a unival subtree.
def helper(root):
    if root is None:
        return 0, True

    left_count, is_left_unival = helper(root.left)
    right_count, is_right_unival = helper(root.right)
    total_count = left_count + right_count

    if is_left_unival and is_right_unival:
        if root.left is not None and root.value != root.left.value:
            return total_count, False
        if root.right is not None and root.value != root.right.value:
            return total_count, False
        return total_count + 1, True

    return total_count, False
```

6.2 Reconstruct tree from pre-order and in-order traversals

Given pre-order and in-order traversals of a binary tree, write a function to reconstruct the tree.

For example, given the following pre-order traversal:

```
[a, b, d, e, c, f, g]
```

And the following in-order traversal:

```
[d, b, e, a, f, c, g]
```

You should return the following tree:

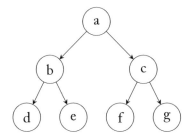

Solution

Recall the definitions of pre-order and in-order traversals:

For pre-order:

- Evaluate root node
- Evaluate left child node recursively

- Evaluate right child node recursively

For in-order:

- Evaluate left child node recursively
- Evaluate root node
- Evaluate right child node recursively

Let's consider the given example again.

Notice that because we always evaluate the root node first in a pre-order traversal, the first element in the pre-order traversal will always be the root. The second element is then either the root of the left child node if there is one, or the root of the right child node. But how do we know?

We can look at the in-order traversal.

Because we look at the left child node first in an in-order traversal, all the elements up until the root will be part of the left subtree. All elements after the root will be the right subtree.

Pre-order:

a	b	d	e	c	f	g
r	left			right		

In-order:

d	b	e	a	f	c	g
left			r	right		

(r = root)

This gives us an idea for how to solve the problem:

- Find the root by looking at the first element in the pre-order traversal

CHAPTER 6. TREES

- Find out how many elements are in the left subtree and right subtree by searching for the index of the root in the in-order traversal

- Recursively reconstruct the left subtree and right subtree

The code for this problem would look like this:

```python
def reconstruct(preorder, inorder):
    if not preorder and not inorder:
        return None

    if len(preorder) == len(inorder) == 1:
        return preorder[0]

    # We assume that elements of the input lists are tree nodes.
    root = preorder[0]
    root_i = inorder.index(root)
    root.left = reconstruct(preorder[1:1 + root_i],
                            inorder[0:root_i])
    root.right = reconstruct(preorder[1 + root_i:],
                             inorder[root_i + 1:])

    return root
```

6.3 Evaluate arithmetic tree

Suppose an arithmetic expression is given as a binary tree. Each leaf is an integer and each internal node is one of +, -, *, or /.

Given the root to such a tree, write a function to evaluate it.

For example, given the following tree:

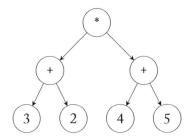

You should return 45, as it is (3 + 2) * (4 + 5).

Solution

This type of tree is more formally known as an expression tree, and we can use a form of post-order traversal to evaluate it. We start by checking the value of the root node. If it is one of the four operators described above, we recursively find the value of the node's left and right children and apply the operator to them.

If it is not an arithmetic operator, the node must contain a number, which we can simply return.

```
class Node:
    def __init__(self, data, left=None, right=None):
        self.data = data
        self.left = left
        self.right = right

PLUS = "+"
MINUS = "-"
TIMES = "*"
DIVIDE = "/"

def evaluate(root):
    if root.data == PLUS:
        return evaluate(root.left) + evaluate(root.right)
    elif root.data == MINUS:
        return evaluate(root.left) - evaluate(root.right)
    elif root.data == TIMES:
        return evaluate(root.left) * evaluate(root.right)
```

CHAPTER 6. TREES

```
    elif root.data == DIVIDE:
        return evaluate(root.left) / evaluate(root.right)
    else:
        return root.val
```

This algorithm runs in $\mathcal{O}(n)$ time and $\mathcal{O}(h)$ space, since we must traverse all nodes and our stack will hold at most a number of elements equal to the tree's height.

6.4 Get tree level with minimum sum

Given a binary tree, return the level of the tree that has the minimum sum. The level of a node is defined as the number of connections required to get to the root, with the root having level zero.

For example:

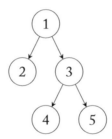

In this tree, level 0 has sum 1, level 1 has sum 5, and level 2 has sum 9, so the level with the minimum sum is 0.

Solution

In order to calculate the sum of each level, we would like to iterate over this tree level by level. Unfortunately, none of the traversal methods we discuss in the introduction seem to achieve this. An in-order traversal might work for the example described above, but it would fail if Node(2) had a child.

Instead, we can use a queue to ensure that each node is dealt is processed in the correct order. More concretely, items in our queue will be tuples containing the value and level for a given node. Each time we pop an element from the queue, we add to the total for the corresponding level and add any child nodes to the end of the queue, with an incremented level.

We will keep track of the sum in each level using a dictionary, allowing us to store both positive and negative values.

```python
from collections import defaultdict, deque

class Node:
    def __init__(self, data, left=None, right=None):
        self.data = data
        self.left = left
        self.right = right

def smallest_level(root):
    queue = deque([])
    queue.append((root, 0))

    # Create a map to accumulate the sum for each level.
    level_to_sum = defaultdict(int)

    while queue:
        node, level = queue.popleft()
        level_to_sum[level] += node.data

        if node.right:
            queue.append((node.right, level + 1))

        if node.left:
            queue.append((node.left, level + 1))

    return min(level_to_sum, key=level_to_sum.get)
```

The time complexity for this function is $\mathcal{O}(n)$.

7

Binary Search Trees

A binary search tree, or BST, is a binary tree whose node values are guaranteed to stay in sorted order; that is, an in-order traversal of its nodes will create a sorted list. For example, here is a BST of integers rooted at 7:

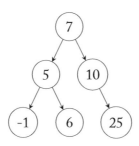

Similar to how a sorted array offers more efficient search times over unsorted arrays, BSTs provide several improvements over standard binary trees.

In particular, `insert`, `find`, and `delete` operations all run in $\mathcal{O}(h)$ time, where h is the height of the tree. If an efficient implementation is used to maintain the height of the tree around $\mathcal{O}(\log n)$, where n is the number of nodes, then these operations will all be logarithmic in n.

A simple Python BST can be written as follows:

```python
class Node:
    def __init__(self, data, left=None, right=None):
        self.data = data
        self.left = left
        self.right = right

class BST:
    def __init__(self):
        self.root = None

    def insert(self, x):
        if not self.root:
            self.root = Node(x)
        else:
            self._insert(x, self.root)

    def _insert(self, x, root):
        if x < root.data:
            if not root.left:
                root.left = Node(x)
            else:
                self.insert(x, root.left)
        else:
            if not root.right:
                root.right = Node(x)
            else:
                self.insert(x, root.right)

    def find(self, x):
        if not self.root:
            return False
        else:
            return self._find(x, self.root)

    def _find(self, x, root):
        if not root:
            return False
        elif x == root.data:
            return True
        elif x < root.data:
            return self._find(x, root.left)
        else:
```

```
            return self._find(x, root.right)
```

Note that, as is common in recursive implementations, we use a helper function to properly define our `insert` and `find` methods.

The most common questions on binary search trees will ask you to search for elements, add and remove elements, and determine whether a tree is indeed a BST. We'll cover most of these in the problems to come.

7.1 Find floor and ceiling

Given a binary search tree, find the floor and ceiling of a given integer. The floor is the highest element in the tree less than or equal to an integer, while the ceiling is the lowest element in the tree greater than or equal to an integer.

If either value does not exist, return `None`.

Solution

Under the hood, this problem is closely related to that of checking whether an element exists in a binary search tree.

In that case, we would proceed recursively, starting from the root and comparing each node we hit to the value we are searching for. If the value is less than the node data, we search the left child; if the value is greater, we search the right child. Finally, if we reach a leaf node and still have not found the element, we return `None`.

This problem is not too different, in fact. Our recursive function will have two extra parameters, `floor` and `ceil`, which will initially be defined as `None`. At each node, we can update these parameters as follows:

- If `value < node.data`, we know the ceiling can be no greater than `node.data`
- If `value > node.data`, we know the floor can be no less than `node.data`

Once updated, we continue as before, calling our function recursively on the appropriate child node. At the end, when we reach a leaf node, we return the latest and most accurate values for these parameters.

```python
class Node:
    def __init__(self, data, left=None, right=None):
        self.data = data
        self.left = left
        self.right = right

def get_bounds(root, x, floor=None, ceil=None):
    if not root:
        return floor, ceil

    if x == root.data:
        return x, x

    elif x < root.data:
        floor, ceil = get_bounds(root.left, x, floor, root.data)

    elif x > root.data:
        floor, ceil = get_bounds(root.right, x, root.data, ceil)

    return floor, ceil
```

This algorithm requires a single traversal from the top to the bottom of the tree. Therefore, the time complexity will be $\mathcal{O}(h)$, where h is the height of the tree. If the tree is balanced, this is equal to $\mathcal{O}(\log n)$. Similarly, the space complexity will be $\mathcal{O}(h)$, since we will need to make space on the stack for each recursive call.

7.2 Convert sorted array to BST

Given a sorted array, convert it into a height-balanced binary search tree.

CHAPTER 7. BINARY SEARCH TREES

Solution

If the tree did not have to be balanced, we could initialize the first element as the root of the tree, and add each subsequent element as a right child.

However, as mentioned in the introduction, keeping a binary search tree balanced is crucial to ensuring the efficiency of its operations.

Instead, since the list is sorted, we know that the root should be the element in the middle of the list, which we can call M. Furthermore, the left subtree will be equivalent to a balanced binary search tree created from the first $M - 1$ elements in the list. Analogously, the right subtree can be constructed from the elements after M in our input.

Therefore, we can create this tree recursively by calling our function on successively smaller input ranges to create each subtree.

```python
class Node:
    def __init__(self, data, left=None, right=None):
        self.data = data
        self.left = left
        self.right = right

def make_bst(array):
    if not array:
        return None

    mid = len(array) // 2

    root = Node(array[mid])
    root.left = make_bst(array[:mid])
    root.right = make_bst(array[mid + 1:])

    return root
```

This algorithm will take $\mathcal{O}(n)$ time and space, since for each element of the list, we must construct a node and add it as a child to the tree, each of which can be considered $\mathcal{O}(1)$ operations.

7.3 Construct all BSTs with n nodes

Given an integer n, construct all possible binary search trees with n nodes where all values from [1, ..., n] are used.

For example, given $n = 3$, return the following trees:

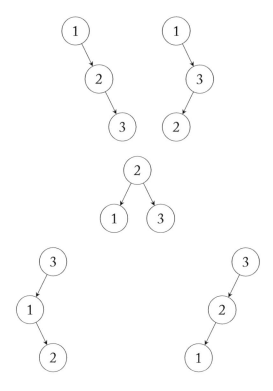

Solution

As with many tree problems, we can formulate this recursively. Let the range of values that nodes in a tree can take be bounded by low and high. If the root of the tree is i, the left subtree will hold data between low and i - 1, and the right subtree will hold data between i + 1 and high.

For each possible value in the left subtree, we can choose one, say j, to be the root, which will again determine what data its left and right children can hold. This process continues until there are no more values to choose.

CHAPTER 7. BINARY SEARCH TREES

Here is what the left subtrees would look like if $n = 5$ and we start by choosing $i = 3$ as our root node.

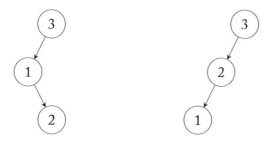

At the same time, an analogous process can be carried out to find all the possible right subtrees.

Finally, for every possible root value, and every possible left and right subtree, we create a node with this value and the corresponding left and right children, and add this node to our list of possible trees.

```
class Node:
    def __init__(self, data, left=None, right=None):
        self.data = data
        self.left = left
        self.right = right

def make_trees(low, high):
    trees = []

    if low > high:
        trees.append(None)
        return trees

    for i in range(low, high + 1):
        left = make_trees(low, i - 1)
        right = make_trees(i + 1, high)

        for l in left:
            for r in right:
                node = Node(i, left=l, right=r)
                trees.append(node)
```

```
        return trees
```

To print out the tree, we can perform a preorder traversal.

```
def preorder(root):
    result = []

    if root:
        result.append(root.data)
        result += preorder(root.left)
        result += preorder(root.right)

    return result
```

Putting it all together, for a given input n, we first construct all trees that use values between 1 and n, and then iterate over each tree to print the nodes.

```
def construct_trees(N):
    trees = make_trees(1, N)
    for tree in trees:
        print(preorder(tree))
```

The number of possible binary search trees grows exponentially with the size of n, as can be seen by inspecting the first few values: 1, 2, 5, 14, 42, 132, 429, 1430, ... In fact, this sequence is defined by the Catalan numbers, which appear in a variety of combinatorial problems.

In any case, `make_trees` takes $\mathcal{O}(n)$ time to build each possible tree, so with an exponential number of trees, this algorithm will run in $\mathcal{O}(n \times 2^n)$ time. Since each tree takes $\mathcal{O}(n)$ space to store its nodes, the space complexity is $\mathcal{O}(n \times 2^n)$ as well.

8

Tries

The first thing to know about a trie is that it is pronounced "try", not "tree".

With that out of the way, a trie is a kind of tree whose nodes typically represent strings, where every descendant of a node shares a common prefix. For this reason tries are often referred to as prefix trees. Here is an example:

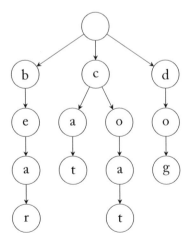

Following all paths from the root to each leaf spells out all the words that this trie contains, in this case "bear", "cat", "coat", and "dog".

There are two main methods used with tries:

- `insert(word)`: add a word to the trie

- `find(word)`: check if a word or prefix exists in the trie

Each of these methods will run in $\mathcal{O}(k)$, where k is the length of the word.

Tries can be implemented in several ways, but in an interview setting the simplest way is to use a nested dictionary, where each key maps to a dictionary whose keys are successive letters in a given word.

Printing out the underlying trie in the image above, we would obtain the following dictionary:

```
{'d':
    {'o':
        {'g': {'#': True}}},
    {'i':
        {'n':
            {'g':
                {'o': {'#': True}}}}},
 'z':
    {'e':
        {'b':
            {'r':
                {'a': {'#': True}}}}},
 'c':
     'a':
        {'t': {'#': True}}}
```

We will see several modifications of tries in the coming problems, but you would do well to understand and be ready with the following basic implementation:

```
ENDS_HERE = '#'

class Trie:
    def __init__(self):
        self._trie = {}
```

```python
    def insert(self, text):
        trie = self._trie
        for char in text:
            if char not in trie:
                trie[char] = {}
            trie = trie[char]
        trie[ENDS_HERE] = True

    def find(self, prefix):
        trie = self._trie
        for char in prefix:
            if char in trie:
                trie = trie[char]
            else:
                return None
        return trie
```

Let's now see some tries in action.

8.1 Implement autocomplete system

Implement an autocomplete system. That is, given a query string s and a set of all possible query strings, return all strings in the set that have s as a prefix.

For example, given the query string de and the set of strings [dog, deer, deal], return [deer, deal].

Solution

Autocomplete can be considered a canonical trie-based question: whenever text completion arises in an interview setting, tries should be the first tool you reach for.

For comparison's sake, though, we will explore a more straightforward solution. We can iterate over the dictionary and check if each word starts with our prefix. If so, we add it to our set of results, and then return it once we're done.

```
WORDS = ['dog', 'deer', 'deal']

def autocomplete(s):
    results = set()
    for word in WORDS:
        if word.startswith(s):
            results.add(word)
    return results
```

This runs in $\mathcal{O}(n)$ time, where n is the number of words in the dictionary.

Fortunately, we can improve on this with a trie. The first step is to insert each word in our dictionary into our trie, using the `insert` method outlined above. For the given words, this would result in the following diagram:

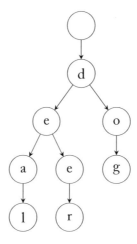

To find all words beginning with "de", we would search from the root along the path from "d" to "e", and then collect all the words under this prefix node. We also make use of the # terminal value to mark whether or not "de" is actually a word in our dictionary or not.

While the worst-case runtime would still be $\mathcal{O}(n)$ if all the search results have that prefix, if the words are uniformly distributed across the alphabet, it should be much faster on average since we no longer have to evaluate words that don't start with our prefix.

```python
ENDS_HERE = '#'

class Trie:
    def __init__(self):
        self._trie = {}

    def insert(self, text):
        trie = self._trie
        for char in text:
            if char not in trie:
                trie[char] = {}
            trie = trie[char]
        trie[ENDS_HERE] = True

    def find(self, prefix):
        trie = self._trie
        for char in prefix:
            if char in trie:
                trie = trie[char]
            else:
                return []
        return self._elements(trie)

    def _elements(self, d):
        result = []
        for c, v in d.items():
            if c == ENDS_HERE:
                subresult = ['']
            else:
                subresult = [c + s for s in self._elements(v)]
            result.extend(subresult)
        return result

trie = Trie()
for word in words:
    trie.insert(word)

def autocomplete(s):
    suffixes = trie.find(s)
    return [s + w for w in suffixes]
```

8.2 Create PrefixMapSum class

Implement a `PrefixMapSum` class with the following methods:

- `insert(key: str, value: int)`: Set a given key's value in the map. If the key already exists, overwrite the value.

- `sum(prefix: str)`: Return the sum of all values of keys that begin with a given prefix.

For example, you should be able to run the following code:

```
mapsum.insert("columnar", 3)
assert mapsum.sum("col") == 3

mapsum.insert("column", 2)
assert mapsum.sum("col") == 5
```

Solution

Depending on how efficient we want our `insert` and `sum` operations to be, there can be several solutions.

If we care about making `insert` as fast as possible, we can use a simple dictionary to store the value of each key inserted. As a result insertion will be $\mathcal{O}(1)$. Then, if we want to find the `sum` for a given key, we would need to add up the values for every word that begins with that prefix. If n is the number of words inserted so far, and k is the length of the prefix, this will be $\mathcal{O}(n \times k)$.

This could be implemented as follows:

```
class PrefixMapSum:
    def __init__(self):
        self.map = {}
```

CHAPTER 8. TRIES

```python
    def insert(self, key: str, value: int):
        self.map[key] = value

    def sum(self, prefix):
        return sum(value for key, value in self.map.items()
            if key.startswith(prefix))
```

On the other hand, perhaps we will rarely be inserting new words, and need our sum retrieval to be very efficient. In this case, every time we insert a new key, we can recompute all its prefixes, so that finding a given sum will be $\mathcal{O}(1)$. However, insertion will take $\mathcal{O}(k^2)$, since slicing is $\mathcal{O}(k)$ and we must do this k times.

```python
from collections import defaultdict

class PrefixMapSum:
    def __init__(self):
        self.map = defaultdict(int)
        self.words = set()

    def insert(self, key: str, value: int):
        # If the key already exists, increment prefix totals
        # by the difference of old and new values.
        if key in self.words:
            value -= self.map[key]
        self.words.add(key)

        for i in range(1, len(key) + 1):
            self.map[key[:i]] += value

    def sum(self, prefix):
        return self.map[prefix]
```

A solution with the best of both options is to use trie data structure. In fact, whenever a problem involves prefixes, a trie should be one of your go-to options.

When we insert a word into the trie, we associate each letter with a dictionary that stores the letters that come after it in various words, as well as the total at any given time.

For example, suppose that we wanted to perform the following operations:

```
mapsum.insert("bag", 4)
mapsum.insert("bath", 5)
```

For the first `insert` call, since there is nothing already in the trie, we would create the following:

```
{"b": "total": 4,
    {"a": "total": 4,
        {"g": "total": 4}
    }
}
```

When we next insert `bath`, we will step letter by letter through the trie, incrementing the total for the prefixes already in the trie, and adding new totals for prefixes that do not exist. The resulting dictionary would look like this:

```
{"b": "total": 9,
    {"a": "total": 9,
        {"g": "total": 4},
        {"t": "total": 5,
            {"h": "total": 5}
        }
    }
}
```

As a result, `insert` and `sum` will involve stepping through the dictionary a number of times equal to the length of the prefix. Since finding the dictionary values at each level is constant time, this algorithm is $\mathcal{O}(k)$ for both methods.

```
from collections import defaultdict
```

```
class TrieNode:
    def __init__(self):
        self.letters = {}
        self.total = 0

class PrefixMapSum:
    def __init__(self):
        self._trie = TrieNode()
        self.map = {}

    def insert(self, key, value):
        # If the key already exists, increment prefix totals by
        # the difference of old and new values.
        value -= self.map.get(key, 0)
        self.map[key] = value

        trie = self._trie
        for char in key:
            if char not in trie.letters:
                trie.letters[char] = TrieNode()
            trie = trie.letters[char]
            trie.total += value

    def sum(self, prefix):
        d = self._trie
        for char in prefix:
            if char in d.letters:
                d = d.letters[char]
            else:
                return 0
        return d.total
```

8.3   Find Maximum XOR of element pairs

Given an array of integers, find the maximum XOR of any two elements.

CHAPTER 8. TRIES

Solution

One solution here would be to loop over each pair of integers and XOR them, keeping track of the maximum found so far. If there are n numbers, this would take $\mathcal{O}(n^2)$ time.

We can improve on this by using a trie data structure. If we represent each integer as a binary number with k bits, we can insert it into a trie with its most significant bit at the top and each successive bit one level down. For example, 4, 6, and 7 could be represented in a three-level trie as follows:

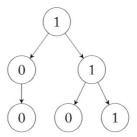

Why would we want to do this? Well, once we have constructed such a trie, we can find the maximum XOR product for any given element by going down the trie and always trying to take the path with an opposite bit.

For example, suppose we wanted to find the maximum XOR for 2, which we will represent as 010, using the trie above. We would use the following procedure:

- The first bit is 0, so we look for a node on the top level with the value 1. Since this exists, we make this our current node, and increment our XOR value by 1 << 2.

- Next, since the second bit is 1, we want to find a child node with the value 0. Again, this exists, so we move down to 0, and increment our XOR value by 1 << 1.

- Finally, the last bit is 0, so we look for a child node with a value of 1. This does not exist, however, so we do not increment our count.

CHAPTER 8. TRIES

After traversing the trie, we would find the maximum XOR to be 1 << 2 + 1 << 1, or 6.

These trie operations can be implemented as shown below:

```python
class Trie:
    def __init__(self, k):
        self._trie = {}
        self.size = k

    def insert(self, item):
        trie = self._trie

        for i in range(self.size, -1, -1):
            bit = bool(item & (1 << i))
            if bit not in trie:
                trie[bit] = {}
            trie = trie[bit]

    def find_max_xor(self, item):
        trie = self._trie
        xor = 0

        for i in range(self.size, -1, -1):
            bit = bool(item & (1 << i))
            if (1 - bit) in trie:
                xor |= (1 << i)
                trie = trie[1 - bit]
            else:
                trie = trie[bit]

        return xor
```

Putting it all together, our solution is to first instantiate a `Trie`, using the maximum bit length to determine the size. Then, we insert the binary representation of each element into the trie. Finally, we loop over each integer to find the maximum XOR that can be generated, updating an XOR counter if the result is the greatest seen so far.

```
def find_max_xor(array):
    k = max(array).bit_length()
    trie = Trie(k)

    for i in array:
        trie.insert(i)

    xor = 0
    for i in array:
        xor = max(xor, trie.find_max_xor(i))

    return xor
```

The complexity of each `insert` and `find_max_xor` operation is $\mathcal{O}(k)$, where k is the number of bits in the maximum element of the array. Since we must perform these operations for every element, this algorithm takes $\mathcal{O}(n \times k)$ time overall. Similarly, because our trie holds N words of size k, this uses $\mathcal{O}(n \times k)$ space.

9

Heaps

We now build on our foundation of tree knowledge by exploring heaps. A heap is a tree that satisfied the (aptly named) heap property, which comes in two flavors:

- In a max-heap, the parent node's value is always greater than or equal to its child node(s)
- In a min-heap, the parent node's value is always smaller than or equal to its child node(s)

Note that, unlike with BSTs, it is possible for a left child to have a greater value (in the case of a min-heap) or for a right child to have a smaller value (in the case of a max-heap).

While it is possible for parent nodes to have more than two children, almost all interview questions will deal with binary heaps, so we will make that assumption throughout the following problems. In the following explanation we will also assume that we are dealing with a min-heap, but the same principles apply for max-heaps.

For example, here is a heap of integers:

CHAPTER 9. HEAPS

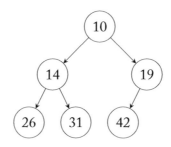

We can also represent a heap in a more space-efficient way by using an array. In this style, the two child nodes of a parent node located at index i can be found at indices $2i + 1$ and $2i + 2$, like so:

| 10 | 14 | 19 | 26 | 31 | 42 |

When using an array to represent a heap, the heap must be filled in level by level, left to right.

Whenever you are asked to find the top k or minimum k values, a heap should be the first thing that comes to mind. Heaps are closely tied to the heapsort sorting algorithm, priority queue implementations, and graph algorithms such as Dijkstra's algorithm, which we will explore in later chapters.

You should be familiar with the following heap operations:

- `insert(heap, x)`: add an element x to the heap, $\mathcal{O}(\log n)$
- `delete-min(heap)`: remove the lowest node, $\mathcal{O}(\log n)$
- `heapify(array)`: convert an array into a heap by repeated insertions, $\mathcal{O}(n \log n)$

In the solutions that follow we will make use of Python's `heapq` module to implement the methods above. The corresponding operations are as follows:

- `heapq.heappush(heap, x)`
- `heapq.heappop(heap)`

- `heapq.heapify(array)`

Let's jump in.

9.1 Compute the running median

Compute the running median of a sequence of numbers. That is, given a stream of numbers, print out the median of the list so far after each new element.

Recall that the median of an even-numbered list is the average of the two middle numbers.

For example, given the sequence [2, 1, 5, 7, 2, 0, 5], your algorithm should print out:

```
2
1.5
2
3.5
2
2
2
```

Solution

In the introduction we learned that finding minimal and maximal values are great reasons to use heaps. But how do they apply to finding medians?

For this problem, we need to think outside the box and use two heaps: a min-heap and a max-heap. We will keep all elements smaller than the median in the max-heap and all elements larger than the median in the min-heap. As long as we keep these heaps the same size, we can guarantee that the median is either the root of the min-heap or the max-heap (or both).

Whenever we encounter a new element from the stream, we will first add it to one of our heaps: the max-heap if the element is smaller than the median, or the min-heap if it is bigger. If both heaps are of equal size, we will arbitrarily choose to add to the max-heap.

Then we re-balance if necessary by moving the root of the larger heap to the smaller one. This is only necessary if one heap is larger than the other by more than 1 element.

Finally, we can print out our median. This will either be the root of the larger heap, or the average of the two roots if they're of equal size.

```python
import heapq

def get_median(min_heap, max_heap):
    if len(min_heap) > len(max_heap):
        min_val = heapq.heappop(min_heap)
        heapq.heappush(min_heap, min_val)
        return min_val
    elif len(min_heap) < len(max_heap):
        max_val = heapq.heappop(max_heap)
        heapq.heappush(max_heap, max_val)
        return max_val
    else:
        min_val = heapq.heappop(min_heap)
        heapq.heappush(min_heap, min_val)
        max_val = heapq.heappop(max_heap)
        heapq.heappush(max_heap, max_val)
        return (min_val + max_val) / 2

def add(num, min_heap, max_heap):
    # If empty, then just add it to the max heap.
    if len(min_heap) + len(max_heap) <= 1:
        heapq.heappush(max_heap, num)
        return

    median = get_median(min_heap, max_heap)
    if num > median:
        # add it to the min heap
        heapq.heappush(min_heap, num)
    else:
```

```
            heapq.heappush(max_heap, num)

def rebalance(min_heap, max_heap):
    if len(min_heap) > len(max_heap) + 1:
        root = heapq.heappop(min_heap)
        heapq.heappush(max_heap, root)
    elif len(max_heap) > len(min_heap) + 1:
        root = heapq.heappop(max_heap)
        heapq.heappush(min_heap, root)

def print_median(min_heap, max_heap):
    print(get_median(min_heap, max_heap))

def running_median(stream):
    min_heap = []
    max_heap = []
    for num in stream:
        add(num, min_heap, max_heap)
        rebalance(min_heap, max_heap)
        print_median(min_heap, max_heap)
```

The running time for this algorithm is $\mathcal{O}(n \log n)$, since for each element we perform a constant number of heappush and heappop operations, each of which take $\mathcal{O}(\log n)$ in the worst case.

9.2 Find most similar websites

You are given a list of (website, user) pairs that represent users visiting websites. Come up with a program that identifies the top k pairs of websites with the greatest similarity.

For example, suppose $k = 1$, and the list of tuples is:

```
[('google.com', 1), ('google.com', 3), ('google.com', 5),
 ('pets.com', 1), ('pets.com', 2), ('yahoo.com', 6),
 ('yahoo.com', 2), ('yahoo.com', 3), ('yahoo.com', 4), ('yahoo.com', 5)
 ('wikipedia.org', 4), ('wikipedia.org', 5), ('wikipedia.org', 6),
```

```
('wikipedia.org', 7), ('bing.com', 1), ('bing.com', 3), ('bing.com': 5),
('bing.com', 6)]
```

To compute the similarity between two websites you should compute the number of users they have in common divided by the number of users who have visited either site in total. (This is known as the Jaccard index.)

For example, in this case, we would conclude that google.com and bing.com are the most similar, with a score of $3/4$, or 0.75.

Solution

First, let's implement the similarity metric defined above as a helper function.

```
def compute_similarity(a, b, visitors):
    return len(visitors[a] & visitors[b]) / len(visitors[a] | visitors[b])
```

This function relies on our ability to quickly find all the visitors for a given website. Therefore, we should first iterate through our input and build a hash table that maps websites to sets of users.

Following this, we can consider each pair of websites and compute its similarity measure. Since we will need to know the top scores, we can store each value and the pair that generated it in a heap. To keep our memory footprint down, we can ensure that at any given time only the k pairs with the highest scores remain in our heap by popping lower-valued pairs.

Finally, we can return the values that are left in our heap after processing each pair of websites.

```
def top_pairs(log, k):
    visitors = defaultdict(set)
    for site, user in log:
        visitors[site].add(user)
```

```
    pairs = []
    sites = list(visitors.keys())

    for _ in range(k):
        heapq.heappush(pairs, (0, ('', '')))

    for i in range(len(sites) - 1):
        for j in range(i + 1, len(sites)):
            score = compute_similarity(sites[i], sites[j], visitors)
            heapq.heappushpop(pairs, (score, (sites[i], sites[j])))

    return [pair[1] for pair in pairs]
```

For each pair of websites, we must compute the union of its users. As a result, this part of our algorithm will take $\mathcal{O}(n^2 \times m)$, where n is the number of sites and m is the number of users. Inserting into and deleting from the heap is logarithmic in the size of the heap, so if we assume $k < m$, our heap operations will be dominated by the calculation above. Therefore, our time complexity will be $\mathcal{O}(n^2 \times m)$.

As for space complexity, our hash table will require n^2 keys, and our heap will have at most k elements. Assuming $k < n^2$, then, the space required by this program will be $\mathcal{O}(n^2)$.

9.3 Generate regular numbers

A regular number in mathematics is defined as one which evenly divides some power of 60. Equivalently, we can say that a regular number is one whose only prime divisors are 2, 3, and 5.

These numbers have had many applications, from helping ancient Babylonians keep time to tuning instruments according to the diatonic scale.

Given an integer n, write a program that generates, in order, the first n regular numbers.

Solution

A naive solution would be to first generate all powers of 2, 3, and 5 up to some stopping point, and then find every product we can obtain from multiplying one power from each group. We can then sort these products and take the first n to find our solution.

```python
def regular_numbers(n):
    twos = [2 ** i for i in range(n)]
    threes = [3 ** i for i in range(n)]
    fives = [5 ** i for i in range(n)]

    solution = set()
    for two in twos:
        for three in threes:
            for five in fives:
                solution.add(two * three * five)

    return sorted(solution)[:n]
```

Since there are n integers in each prime group, our solution set will contain $\mathcal{O}(n^3)$ numbers. As a result, the sorting process will take $\mathcal{O}(n^3 \log n)$ time.

Note that in the above solution, we had to sort all the multiples at the end. If we were able to just keep track of the smallest N multiples at any given point, we could make this solution significantly more efficient. It sounds like this is a perfect use case for a heap!

For any regular number x, we can generate three additional regular numbers by calculating $2x$, $3x$, and $5x$. Conversely, it must be the case that any regular number must be twice, three times, or five times some other regular number.

To take advantage of this, we can initialize a min-heap starting with the value 1. Each time we pop a value x from the heap, we yield it, then push $2x$, $3x$, and $5x$ onto the heap. We can continue this process until we have yielded N integers.

One point to consider is that, for example, the number 6 will be pushed to the heap twice, once for being a multiple of two and once for being a multiple of three. To avoid yielding this value twice, we maintain a variable for the last number popped, and only process a value if it is greater than this variable.

```
import heapq

def regular_numbers(n):
    solution = [1]
    last = 0; count = 0

    while count < n:
        x = heapq.heappop(solution)
        if x > last:
            yield x
            last = x; count += 1
        heapq.heappush(solution, 2 * x)
        heapq.heappush(solution, 3 * x)
        heapq.heappush(solution, 5 * x)
```

Each pop and push operation will take $\mathcal{O}(\log n)$ time. Since we will consider at most the first n multiples of 2, 3, and 5, there will be $\mathcal{O}(n)$ of these operations, leading to an $\mathcal{O}(n \log n)$ runtime.

Now let's try something a little more complicated.

9.4 Build a Huffman tree

Huffman coding is a method of encoding characters based on their frequency. Each letter is assigned a variable-length binary string, such as `0101` or `111110`, where shorter lengths correspond to more common letters. To accomplish this, a binary tree is built such that the path from the root to any leaf uniquely maps to a character. When traversing the path, descending to a left child corresponds to a `0` in the prefix, while descending right corresponds to `1`.

Here is an example tree (note that only the leaf nodes have letters):

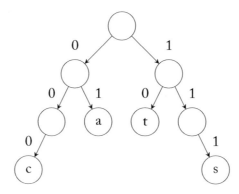

With this encoding, "cats" would be represented as 0000110111.

Given a dictionary of character frequencies, build a Huffman tree, and use it to determine a mapping between characters and their encoded binary strings.

Solution

First note that regardless of how we build the tree, we would like each leaf node to represent a character.

```
class Node:
    def __init__(self, char, left=None, right=None):
        self.char = char
        self.left = left
        self.right = right
```

When building the tree, we should try to ensure that less frequent characters end up further away from the root. We can accomplish this as follows:

- Start by initializing one node for each letter.

- Create a new node whose children are the two least common letters, and whose value is the sum of their frequencies.

- Continuing in this way, take each node, in order of increasing letter frequency, and combine it with another node.

CHAPTER 9. HEAPS

- When there is a path from the root to each character, stop.

For example, suppose our letter frequencies were {"a": 3, "c": 6, "e": 8, "f": 2}.

The stages to create our tree would be as follows:

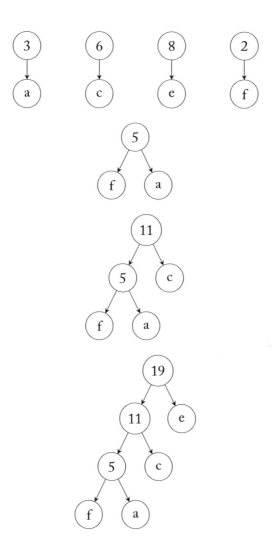

In order to efficiently keep track of node values, we can use a priority queue. We will repeatedly pop the two least common letters, create a combined node, and push that node back onto the queue.

```
import heapq

def build_tree(frequencies):
    nodes = []
    for char, frequency in frequencies.items():
        heapq.heappush(nodes, (frequency, Node(char)))

    while len(nodes) > 1:
        f1, n1 = heapq.heappop(nodes)
        f2, n2 = heapq.heappop(nodes)
        node = Node('*', left=n1, right=n2)
        heapq.heappush(nodes, (f1 + f2, node))

    root = nodes[0][1]

    return root
```

Each pop and push operation takes $\mathcal{O}(\log n)$ time, so building this tree will be $\mathcal{O}(n \log n)$, where n is the number of characters.

Finally, we must use the tree to create our encoding. This can be done recursively: starting with the root, we traverse each path of the tree, while keeping track of a running string. Each time we descend left, we add 0 to this string, and each time we descend right, we add 1. Whenever we reach a leaf node, we assign the current value of the string to the character at that node.

```
def encode(root, string='', mapping={}):
    if not root:
        return

    if not root.left and not root.right:
        mapping[root.char] = string

    encode(root.left, string + '0', mapping)
    encode(root.right, string + '1', mapping)

    return mapping
```

As a result, the encoding for the tree above will be {"f": 000, "a": 001, "c": 01, "e": 1}.

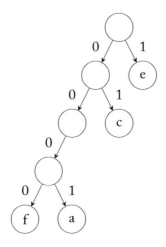

It will take, on average, $\mathcal{O}(\log n)$ time to traverse the path to any character, so encoding a string of length m using this tree will take $\mathcal{O}(m \log n)$.

10

Graphs

Graphs are one of the most important and widely used data structures. Website links, friend connections, and map routes all rely on graph representations, along with countless other applications.

Formally, graphs are defined as a set of vertices connected by edges. If these edges go in one direction, the graph is said to be **directed**; otherwise it is **undirected**. Each edge can additionally be associated with a number that represents its "cost" or "benefit".

An example of a directed graph would be followers on Twitter. Just because you follow Elon Musk does not mean he follows you back. On the other hand, friend connections on Facebook are undirected.

Mathematicians working in graph theory have names for many different graph concepts. We don't need to know all of them, but a few will be useful for the explanations that follow:

- **neighbor** of X: any vertex connected to X by an edge
- **path**: a route of edges that connects two vertices
- **cycle**: a path that begins and end on the same vertex

CHAPTER 10. GRAPHS

- **directed acyclic graph** (DAG): a directed graph that does not contain any cycles

- **connected graph**: a graph in which there is always a path between any two vertices

Another classic example of a (directed) graph is airline routes. In the following diagram, we see that there are flights between JFK and SFO, ORL and LAX, and so on, and each one has an associated plane ticket cost. This graph has several cycles, since it is indeed possible to start and end at JFK after following several edges.

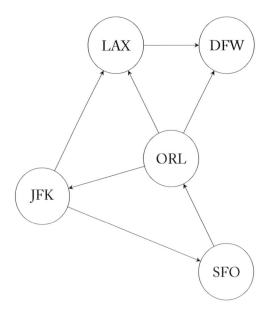

Graphs can be represented in two main ways: adjacency lists and adjacency matrices.

An adjacency list is essentially a dictionary mapping each vertex to the other vertices between which there is an edge. For the airline diagram above this would be as follows:

```
{
    'JFK': ['SFO', 'LAX'],
    'SFO': ['ORL'],
    'ORL': ['JFK', 'LAX', 'DFW'],
```

```
        'LAX': ['DFW']
}
```

On the other hand, in an adjacency matrix, each vertex is associated with a row and column of an $N \times N$ matrix, and `matrix[i][j]` will be 1 if there is an edge from i to j, else 0.

This would look like the following:

```
indices = {
    'JFK': 0,
    'SFO': 1,
    'ORL': 2,
    'LAX': 3,
    'DFW': 4
}

graph = [
    [0, 1, 0, 1, 0],
    [0, 0, 1, 0, 0],
    [1, 0, 0, 1, 1],
    [0, 0, 0, 0, 1],
    [0, 0, 0, 0, 0]
]
```

In general, the adjacency list representation is more space efficient if there are not that many edges (also known as a sparse graph), whereas an adjacency matrix has faster lookup times to check if a given edge exists but uses more space.

You should know the two main traversal methods for graphs: depth-first search (DFS) and breadth-first search (BFS).

Below is a typical DFS implementation. Note the recursive aspect: for each vertex we visit, we call our function again on each of its neighbors.

```
def DFS(graph, start, visited=set()):
    visited.add(start)
```

```
    for neighbor in graph[start]:
        if neighbor not in visited:
            DFS(graph, neighbor, visited)

    return visited
```

BFS, on the other hand, relies on a queue. For each item that we pop off the queue, we find its unvisited neighbors and add them to the end of the queue.

```
from collections import deque

def BFS(graph, start, visited={}):
    queue = deque([start])

    while queue:
        vertex = queue.popleft()
        visited.add(vertex)
        for neighbor in graph[vertex]:
            if neighbor not in visited:
                queue.append(neighbor)

    return visited
```

Both of these algorithms run in $\mathcal{O}(V + E)$ time and $\mathcal{O}(V)$ space in the worst case.

In this chapter we will explore the advantages and disadvantages of each of these traversal methods, as well as a technique for ordering vertices known as topological sort.

10.1 Determine if a cycle exists

Given an undirected graph, determine if it contains a cycle.

Solution

One way to think about this problem is as follows: suppose we are traversing the graph's edges, starting from a given vertex. If, for some vertex, we find that one of its neighbors has already been visited, then we know that there are two ways to reach that neighbor from the same starting point, which indicates a cycle.

We can implement this solution using depth-first search. For each vertex in the graph, if it has not already been visited, we call our search function on it. This function will recursively traverse unvisited neighbors of the vertex, and return True if we come across the situation described above.

If we are able to visit all vertices without finding a duplicate path, we return False.

```
def search(graph, vertex, visited, parent):
    visited[vertex] = True

    for neighbor in graph[vertex]:
        if not visited[neighbor]:
            if search(graph, neighbor, visited, vertex):
                return True

        elif parent != neighbor:
            return True

    return False

def has_cycle(graph):
    visited = {v: False for v in graph.keys()}

    for vertex in graph.keys():
        if not visited[vertex]:
            if search(graph, vertex, visited, None):
                return True

    return False
```

The time complexity of this solution will be $\mathcal{O}(V + E)$, since in the worst case we

CHAPTER 10. GRAPHS

will have to traverse all edges of the graph. Our search will take $\mathcal{O}(V)$ space in the worst case to store the vertices in a given traversal on the stack.

10.2 Remove edges to create even trees

You are given a tree with an even number of nodes. Consider each connection between a parent and child node to be an "edge". You would like to remove some of these edges, such that the disconnected subtrees that remain each have an even number of nodes.

For example, suppose your input is the following tree:

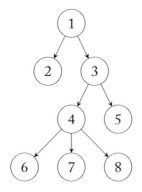

In this case, if we remove the edge (3, 4), both resulting subtrees will be even.

Write a function that returns the **maximum** number of edges you can remove while still satisfying this requirement.

Solution

First note that if a node has an odd number of descendants, we can cut off the link between that node and its parent in order to create an even-sized subtree. Each time we do this, we are left with another even-sized group, to which we can apply the same procedure.

CHAPTER 10. GRAPHS

For example, let's take the example tree above. The lowest edge we can cut is that connecting nodes 3 and 4. Once this is cut, we are left with the following tree:

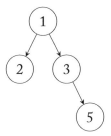

We now see that 3 still has an odd number of descendants, so we can cut the link between 1 and 3. In total, then, we are able to remove two edges.

It is not necessary, however, to remove the edges precisely in this order. Instead, it is sufficient to know that this greedy approach works, so that we can identify all the nodes with an odd number of descendants (except for the root, which cannot be cut off in this way), and increment a counter for each.

Let's assume our input is presented in the form of a graph, like so:

```
graph = {
    1: [2, 3],
    2: [],
    3: [4, 5],
    4: [6, 7, 8],
    5: [],
    6: [],
    7: [],
    8: []
}
```

We will first perform a depth-first search traversal through this graph to populate a dictionary which stores the number of descendants per node. Once this is done, we simply count up how many of these values are odd and return this total.

```
from collections import defaultdict

def traverse(graph, curr, result):
    descendants = 0

    for child in graph[curr]:
        num_nodes, result = traverse(graph, child, result)

        result[child] += num_nodes - 1
        descendants += num_nodes

    return descendants + 1, result

def max_edges(graph):
    start = list(graph)[0]
    vertices = defaultdict(int)

    _, descendants = traverse(graph, start, vertices)

    return len([val for val in descendants.values() if val % 2 == 1])
```

Our tree will have n nodes, so the depth-first search will take $\mathcal{O}(n)$ time. The space complexity is likewise $\mathcal{O}(n)$, since we populate a dictionary with n keys, one for each node.

10.3 Create stepword chain

Given a start word, an end word, and a dictionary of valid words, find the shortest transformation sequence from start to end such that only one letter is changed at each step of the sequence, and each transformed word exists in the dictionary. If there is no possible transformation, return null. Each word in the dictionary has the same length as start and end and is lowercase.

For example, given start = "dog", end = "cat", and dictionary = {"dot", "dop", "dat", "cat"}, return ["dog", "dot", "dat", "cat"].

Given start = "dog", end = "cat", and dictionary = {"dot", "tod", "dat", "dar"}, return null as there is no possible transformation from "dog" to "cat".

Solution

We can model this problem as a graph: the nodes will be the words in the dictionary, and we can form an edge between two nodes if and only if one character can be modified in one word to get to the other.

Then we can do a typical breadth-first search starting from start and finishing once we encounter end:

```
from collections import deque
from string import ascii_lowercase

def word_ladder(start, end, words):
    queue = deque([(start, [start])])

    while queue:
        word, path = queue.popleft()
        if word == end:
            return path

        for i in range(len(word)):
            for char in ascii_lowercase:
                next_word = word[:i] + char + word[i + 1:]
                if next_word in words:
                    words.remove(next_word)
                    queue.append([next_word, path + [next_word]])

    return None
```

This takes $\mathcal{O}(n^2)$ time and $\mathcal{O}(n)$ space.

10.4 Beat Snakes and Ladders

Snakes and Ladders is a game played on a 10×10 board, the goal of which is get from square 1 to square 100. On each turn players will roll a six-sided die and move forward a number of spaces equal to the result. If they land on a square that represents a snake or ladder, they will be transported ahead or behind, respectively, to a new square.

A typical board for Snakes and Ladders looks like this:

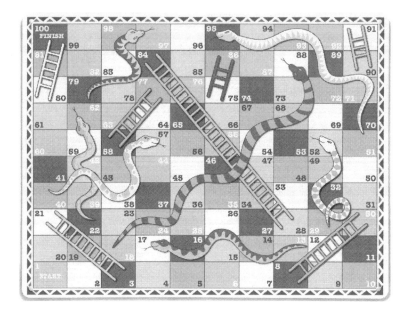

Find the smallest number of turns it takes to play snakes and ladders.

For convenience, here are the squares representing snakes and ladders, and their outcomes:

```
snakes = {17: 13, 52: 29, 57: 40, 62: 22, 88: 18, 95: 51, 97: 79}
ladders = {3: 21, 8: 30, 28: 84, 58: 77, 75: 86, 80: 100, 90: 91}
```

Solution

We know that during each turn a player has six possible moves, advancing from one to six squares. So our first thought might be to recursively try each move, exploring all possible paths. Then, we can return the length of the shortest path.

However, because there are snakes, we would eventually enter a never-ending loop, repeatedly advancing to a snake square and being sent back. Even without this issue, this solution would be exponentially slow, since we have six potential moves at each square.

A more efficient method is to use a version of breadth-first search.

We can maintain a queue of tuples representing the current square and the number of turns taken so far, starting with $(0, 0)$. For each item popped from the queue, we examine the moves that can be made from it. If a move crosses the finish line, we've found a solution. Otherwise, if a move takes us to a square we have not already visited, we add that square to the queue.

The key point here is that squares will only be put in the queue on the earliest turn they can be reached. For example, even though it is possible to reach square 5 by moving $[1, 1, 1, 1, 1]$, the initial move 5 will get there first. So we can guarantee that we will only examine each square once, and that the number of turns associated with each square will be minimal.

```
from collections import deque

def minimum_turns(snakes, ladders):
    # Create a board with the given snakes and ladders.
    board = {square: square for square in range(1, 101)}
    for start, end in snakes.items():
        board[start] = end

    for start, end in ladders.items():
        board[start] = end

    # Perform BFS to reach the last square as quickly as possible.
    start, end = 0, 100
    turns = 0
```

```
        path = deque([(start, turns)])
        visited = set()

        while path:
            square, turns = path.popleft()

            for move in range(square + 1, square + 7):
                if move >= end:
                    return turns + 1

                if move not in visited:
                    visited.add(move)
                    path.append((board[move], turns + 1))
```

Since each square is only placed in the queue once, and our queue operations take constant time, this algorithm is linear in the number of squares.

10.5 Topological sort

We are given a hashmap associating each `courseId` key with a list of `courseIds` values, which tells us that the prerequisites of `courseId` are `courseIds`. Return a sorted ordering of courses such that we can complete the curriculum.

Return null if there is no such ordering.

For example, given the following prerequisites:

```
{
    'CSC300': ['CSC100', 'CSC200'],
    'CSC200': ['CSC100'],
    'CSC100': []
}
```

You should return `['CSC100', 'CSC200', 'CSCS300']`.

CHAPTER 10. GRAPHS

Solution

First, let's understand how the input we are given can be represented in the form of a graph.

Our courses are related to each other by their order, so one promising way would be to make each course a vertex and draw an edge from course A to course B if A is a prerequisite for B.

Once this transformation is complete, our problem becomes one of traversing this directed graph in order to efficiently find out which vertices come before other ones. One technique specially designed to deal with questions like this is known as topological sort.

To gain some context on how topological sort works, let's think about how we would solve this problem manually.

Imagine that we have a to-do list and a result list, and to start our to-do list is populated with all courses that do not have any prerequisites. We can start by taking the first course in our to-do list and moving it to our result list. Next, we remove it as a prerequisite from all its successor courses. If, while we are doing this, some other course finds itself without any prerequisites, we can safely add it to the end of our to-do list.

We can continue this process for each item at the top of our to-do list, and (if it is possible) eventually make our way through the entire order. If in the end we are unable to reach some courses, there must be a circular dependency.

```
from collections import defaultdict, deque

def find_order(course_to_prereqs):
    # Copy list values into a set for faster removal.
    course_to_prereqs = {c: set(p) for c, p in course_to_prereqs.items()}

    # Start off our to-do list with all courses without prerequisites.
    todo = deque([c for c, p in course_to_prereqs.items() if not p])

    # Create a new data structure to map prereqs to successor courses.
```

```python
        prereq_to_courses = defaultdict(list)
        for course, prereqs in course_to_prereqs.items():
            for prereq in prereqs:
                prereq_to_courses[prereq].append(course)

        result = []

        while todo:
            prereq = todo.popleft()
            result.append(prereq)

            # Remove this prereq from all successor courses.
            # If any course now does not have any prereqs, add it to todo.
            for c in prereq_to_courses[prereq]:
                course_to_prereqs[c].remove(prereq)
                if not course_to_prereqs[c]:
                    todo.append(c)

        # Circular dependency
        if len(result) < len(course_to_prereqs):
            return None

        return result
```

Topological sort takes $\mathcal{O}(V + E)$ time and space, where V is the number of vertices and E is the number of edges in our graph.

11

Advanced Data Structures

In the preceding chapters we introduced the data structures that appear most frequently in coding interviews. These are both foundational building blocks of more complicated structures and key ingredients of many of the algorithms that will be considered in Part II.

Of course, we cannot cover the full breadth of this subject, as computer scientists and those in industry have spent years developing data structures optimized for particular applications. Depending on the company, role, and interviewer you may come across a problem that would benefit from a more specialized approach.

In this chapter, we review a few advanced topics that are worth knowing. We recommend becoming familiar with these, at least to the extent of knowing how they work and when they are applicable. Besides allowing you to impress your interviewer, these problems should also give you a glimpse of the wide landscape of data structures.

We first review the Fenwick tree, designed to optimize both updates and range sums in an array. Following this, we take a look at the disjoint-set data structure, which efficiently allows you to partition and merge elements into groups. Finally, we examine the Bloom filter, a probabilistic data structure which quickly checks membership in a set.

Chapter 11. Advanced Data Structures

11.1 Fenwick tree

You are given an array of length 24, where each element represents the number of new subscribers during the corresponding hour. Implement a data structure that efficiently supports the following:

- `update(hour, value)`: Increment the element at index `hour` by `value`.

- `query(start, end)`: Retrieve the number of subscribers that have signed up between `start` and `end` (inclusive).

You can assume that all values get cleared at the end of the day, and that you will not be asked for `start` and end values that wrap around midnight.

Solution

If we look beyond the details, the data structure required here is one that efficiently supports finding the sum of a subarray, and updating individual values in the array. One data structure that fits the bill is a binary indexed tree, or Fenwick tree.

To see how this works, suppose the subscribers for an 8-hour range are as follows: [4, 8, 1, 9, 3, 5, 5, 3], and we wanted to sum up number of subscribers from index 0 to index $n - 1$. A naive solution would require us to go through each element and add it to a running total, which would be $\mathcal{O}(n)$. Instead, if we knew in advance some of the subarray sums, we could break our problem apart into precomputed subproblems. In particular, we can use a technique that relies on binary indexing.

We will create a new array of the same size of our subscriber array, and store values in it as follows:

- If the index is even, simply store the value of `subscribers[i]`.

- If the index is odd, store the sum of a range of values up to i whose length is a power of two.

This is demonstrated in the diagram below, with × representing values of the original array, and arrows representing range sums.

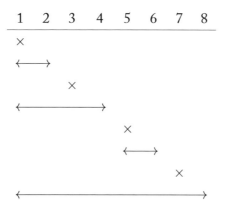

How does this help us? For any range between 0 and $n-1$, we can break it apart into these binary ranges, in such a way that we only require $\mathcal{O}(\log n)$ parts.

To make this more concrete, let's look again at our subscriber array, [4, 8, 1, 9, 3, 5, 5, 3]. For this array, the binary indexed tree would be [4, 12, 1, 22, 3, 8, 5, 38]. As a result, we can calculate query(0, 6) using the following steps:

query(0, 6) = query(0, 3) + query(4, 5) + query(6, 6) = tree[4] + tree[6] + tree[7] = 22 + 8 + 5 = 35.

Note that if our start index is not 0, we can transform our problem from query(a, b) to query(0, b) - query(0, a - 1), so this is applicable for any range.

To find the indices of our tree to sum up, we can use a clever bit manipulation trick. We can find the lowest set bit of a number x by performing x & ~x. Using this, we can keep decrementing the index by the lowest set bit of the current index, until the index gets to zero. We can implement this as follows:

```python
def query(self, index):
    total = 0
    while index > 0:
        total += self.tree[index]
```

```
        index -= index & -index
    return total
```

Now let's take a look at the `update` operation. Changing the value of the 3rd item in the subscriber array from 1 to 2 would change the values of `tree[3]`, `tree[4]`, and `tree[8]`. Again, we can use the "lowest set bit" trick to increment the appropriate indices:

```
def update(self, index, value):
    while index < len(self.tree):
        self.tree[index] += value
        index += index & -index
```

Note that in order for this "trick" to work, we must prepend a zero to our tree array. Otherwise, our `update` operation would never work for the first index, since `0 & -0 = 0`! Essentially, we will change the array to start with an index of one, and modify our function parameters accordingly.

Putting it all together, the code would look like this:

```
class BIT:
    def __init__(self, nums):
        # Prepend a zero to our array to use lowest set bit trick.
        self.tree = [0 for _ in range(len(nums) + 1)]
        for i, num in enumerate(nums):
            self.update(i + 1, num)

    def update(self, index, value):
        while index < len(self.tree):
            self.tree[index] += value
            index += index & -index

    def query(self, index):
        total = 0
        while index > 0:
            total += self.tree[index]
            index -= index & -index
```

```
            return total

class Subscribers:
    def __init__(self, nums):
        self.bit = BIT(nums)
        self.nums = nums

    def update(self, hour, value):
        self.bit.update(hour, value - self.nums[hour])
        self.nums[hour] = value

    def query(self, start, end):
        # Shift start and end indices forward as our array is 1-based.
        return self.bit.query(end + 1) - self.bit.query(start)
```

Because we have decomposed each operation into binary ranges, both update and query are $\mathcal{O}(\log n)$.

11.2 Disjoint-set data structure

A classroom consists of n students, whose friendships can be represented in an adjacency list. For example, the following describes a situation where 0 is friends with 1 and 2, 3 is friends with 6, and so on.

```
{0: [1, 2],
 1: [0, 5],
 2: [0],
 3: [6],
 4: [],
 5: [1],
 6: [3]}
```

Each student can be placed in a friend group, which can be defined as the transitive closure of that student's friendship relations. In other words, this is the smallest set such that no student in the group has any friends outside this group. For the example above, the friend groups would be {0, 1, 2, 5}, {3, 6}, {4}.

Given a friendship list such as the one above, determine the number of friend groups in the class.

Solution

This problem is a classic motivating example for the use of a disjoint-set data structure.

To implement this data structure, we must create two main methods: `union` and `find`. Initially, each student will be in a friend group consisting of only him- or herself. For each friendship in our input, we will call our `union` method to place the two students in the same set. To perform this, we must call `find` to discover which friend group each student is in, and, if they are not the same, assign one student to the friend group of the other.

It may be the case that, after a few `union` calls, friend n may be placed in set $n-1$, friend $n-1$ may be placed in set $n-2$, and so on. As a result, our `find` operation must follow the chain of friend sets until reaching a student who has not been reassigned, which will properly identify the group.

Because the chain we must follow for each `find` call can be n students long, both methods run in $\mathcal{O}(n)$ time. However, with just two minor changes we can cut this runtime down to $\mathcal{O}(1)$ (technically, $\mathcal{O}(\alpha(n))$, where α is the inverse Ackermann function).

The first is called path compression. After we call `find`, we know exactly which group the student belongs to, so we can reassign this student directly to that group. Second, when we unite two students, instead of assigning based on value, we can always assign the student belonging to the smaller set to the larger set. Taken together, these optimizations drastically cut down the time it takes to perform both operations.

```
class DisjointSet:
    def __init__(self, n):
        self.sets = list(range(n))
        self.sizes = [1] * n
        self.count = n

    def union(self, x, y):
```

CHAPTER 11. ADVANCED DATA STRUCTURES

```python
        x, y = self.find(x), self.find(y)
        if x != y:
            # Union by size: always add students to the bigger set.
            if self.sizes[x] < self.sizes[y]:
                x, y = y, x

            self.sets[y] = x
            self.sizes[x] += self.sizes[y]
            self.count -= 1

    def find(self, x):
        group = self.sets[x]

        while group != self.sets[group]:
            group = self.sets[group]

        # Path compression: reassign x to the correct group.
        self.sets[x] = group

        return group
```

With this data structure in place, our solution will be to go through the list of friendships, calling union on each of them. Each time we reassign a student to a different group, we decrement a counter for the number of friend groups, which starts at n. Finally, we return the value of this counter.

```python
def friend_groups(students):
    groups = DisjointSet(len(students))

    for student, friends in students.items():
        for friend in friends:
            groups.union(student, friend)

    return groups.count
```

Since union and find operations are both $O(1)$, the time complexity of this solution is $\mathcal{O}(E)$, where E is the number of edges represented in the adjacency list. We will also use $\mathcal{O}(n)$ space to store the list of assigned friend groups.

11.3 Bloom filter

Implement a data structure which carries out the following operations without resizing the underlying array:

- add(value): add a value to the set of values.

- check(value): check whether a value is in the set.

The check method may return occasional false positives (in other words, incorrectly identifying an element as part of the set), but should always correctly identify a true element.

Solution

While there may be multiple ways of implementing a data structure with these operations, one of the most well-known is called a Bloom filter. A Bloom filter works by hashing each item in multiple ways, so that several values in the array will be set to True for any given input. Then, when we want to check whether a given value has been added, we examine each of the locations that it can be sent to in the hash table, and only return True if all have been set.

To give a simple example, suppose we are dealing with an underlying array of size 100, and have two functions which take in integers as input, defined as follows:

```
def h1(value):
    return ((value + 7) ** 11) % 100

def h2(value):
    return ((value + 11) ** 7) % 100
```

Now suppose we added 3 and 5 to our set. This would involve the following operations:

```
location1 = h1(3) # 0
location2 = h2(3) # 4
array[location1] = array[location2] = True

location1 = h1(5) # 88
location2 = h2(5) # 56
array[location1] = array[location2] = True
```

For most cases this will not cause any problems. However, look what happens when we check 99. Since `h1(99) = 56` and `h2(99) = 0`, both values we check in the array would already be assigned `True`, and we would report this as being in our set.

Although we can reduce the likelihood of this occurring by using more optimal hash functions, and by increasing the initial array size, we cannot get around the fact that a Bloom filter will occasionally return false positives. For this reason it is called a probabilistic data structure.

```
import hashlib

class BloomFilter:
    def __init__(self, n=1000, k=3):
        self.array = [False] * n
        self.hash_algorithms = [
            hashlib.md5,
            hashlib.sha1,
            hashlib.sha256,
            hashlib.sha384,
            hashlib.sha512
        ]
        self.hashes = [self._get_hash(f) for f in self.hash_algorithms[:k]]

    def _get_hash(self, f):
        def hash_function(value):
            h = f(str(value).encode('utf-8')).hexdigest()
            return int(h, 16) % len(self.array)

        return hash_function
```

```python
    def add(self, value):
        for h in self.hashes:
            v = h(value)
            self.array[v] = True

    def check(self, value):
        for h in self.hashes:
            v = h(value)
            if not self.array[v]:
                return False

        return True
```

In the implementation above we maximize the number of hash functions at five, and use built-in cryptographic algorithms that come with Python's `hashlib` library.

Since the number of hashes we must perform for each value is bounded by a constant, and each hash is $\mathcal{O}(1)$, the time complexity of each operation will also be constant. The space complexity will be $\mathcal{O}(n)$, where n is the size of the underlying array.

Part II

Algorithms

12

Recursion

Recursion is one of the core concepts of computer science. It is a powerful technique that involves breaking down a problem into smaller subproblems in order to obtain a solution.

In general, every recursive solution consists of defining two parts:

- The base case: what should the algorithm do in the simplest situation?
- The inductive step: how does the algorithm build up the solution?

A common example is computing the nth Fibonacci number (or computing the nth anything, really, as long as there is a clear method of going from $n-1$ to n).

The base case involving defining the first two Fibonacci numbers, 1 and 1. From here, we define the inductive step, which will apply to every subsequent term:

```
f(n) = f(n - 1) + f(n - 2)
```

A hallmark of every recursive solution is that you call your function on a subset of the input inside the function itself.

To illustrate, here is the full Fibonacci implementation, in only a few lines of code:

```
def fib(n):
    if n <= 1:
        return n
    else:
        return fib(n - 1) + fib(n - 2)
```

A common mistake beginners make is to leave out the base case. Without this, our algorithm would never terminate!

The downside of recursion is that it can be very inefficient: the number of calls to fib in the code above grows exponentially with n! For this reason we will explore improvements to recursive approaches in subsequent chapters such as dynamic programming.

You can bet that most problems involving tree or graph traversal, searching, or backtracking will use some kind of recursion, and even problems that have more optimal solutions will often have a recursive solution that you can rely on in a pinch.

For more details on recursion, see Chapter 12.

12.1 Tower of Hanoi

The Tower of Hanoi is a puzzle game with three rods and n disks, each a different size.

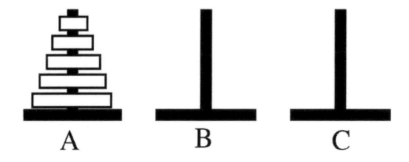

CHAPTER 12. RECURSION

All the disks start off on the first rod in a stack. They are ordered by size, with the largest disk on the bottom and the smallest one at the top.

The goal of this puzzle is to move all the disks from the first rod to the last rod while following these rules:

- You can only move one disk at a time.

- A move consists of taking the uppermost disk from one of the stacks and placing it on top of another stack.

- You cannot place a larger disk on top of a smaller disk.

Write a function that prints out all the steps necessary to complete the Tower of Hanoi. You should assume that the rods are numbered, with the first rod being 1, the second (auxiliary) rod being 2, and the last (goal) rod being 3.

For example, with n = 3, we can do this in 7 moves:

- Move 1 to 3

- Move 1 to 2

- Move 3 to 2

- Move 1 to 3

- Move 2 to 1

- Move 2 to 3

- Move 1 to 3

Solution

The goal of the Tower of Hanoi is to get all n disks from the source peg to the target peg, using a spare peg and abiding by all the constraints. Why does this call for recursion? Note that after some series of moves we will arrive at a new state, hopefully one closer to the solution. We can think of this sequence of states as subproblems to be solved.

As mentioned in the introduction, the first step to any recursive solution is formulating a base case and an inductive case. First let's consider the base cases:

- If there are 0 disks, do nothing, since we are done.
- If there is only 1 disk, we can move it directly from the source peg to the target peg.

Now, let's assume we have an existing `tower_of_hanoi` function that can move n disks from a source peg to a target peg using a spare stack. The recurrence would then look like this:

- If there is more than 1 disk, then we can do the following:
    - Recursively move $n - 1$ disks from the source stack to the spare stack
    - Move the last (biggest) disk from the source stack to the target stack
    - Recursively move all $n - 1$ disks from the spare stack to the target stack

We are able to recursively move the disks because it doesn't break any constraints: we can just treat the base disk as if it weren't there.

In our code, we'll call our source stack a, spare stack b, and target stack c.

```python
def tower_of_hanoi(n, a='1', b='2', c='3'):
    if n >= 1:
        tower_of_hanoi(n - 1, a, c, b)
        print('Move {} to {}'.format(a, c))
        tower_of_hanoi(n - 1, b, a, c)
```

This will run in $\mathcal{O}(2^n)$ time, since for each call we're recursively calling ourselves twice. This should also take $\mathcal{O}(n)$ space since the function call stack goes n calls deep.

12.2 Implement regular expressions

Implement regular expression matching with the following special characters:

- . (period) which matches any single character
- * (asterisk) which matches zero or more of the preceding element

That is, implement a function that takes in a string and a valid regular expression and returns whether or not the string matches the regular expression.

For example, given the regular expression ra. and the string "ray", your function should return True. The same regular expression on the string "raymond" should return False.

Given the regular expression .*at and the string "chat", your function should return true. The same regular expression on the string "chats" should return false.

Solution

Let's think about how we can apply recursion here. Note that if the head of the string matches the head of the regex, we can reduce our problem to comparing the remainders of both. This in fact is a common tactic for finding the inductive step in string problems.

The special characters . and * make implementing this a bit trickier, however, since with * we can match 0 or any number of characters in the beginning.

The basic idea, then, is to do the following. Let's call the string we want to match s and the regex r. Our base case here will be when r is empty, in which we can return True if s is also empty, and False otherwise.

For the inductive step, let's first consider the case where the first character in r is not succeeded by a *. In this situation, we can safely compare the first character of both r and s. If these match, we recursively continue to analyze match(r[1:], s[1:]). Otherwise, we can return False.

Finally, if the first character in r is i fact succeeded by a *, we can try every suffix substring of s on $r[2:]$ and return True if any of them provide a working solution.

The code should look something like this:

```python
def matches_first_char(s, r):
    return s[0] == r[0] or (r[0] == '.' and len(s) > 0)

def matches(s, r):
    if r == '':
        return s == ''

    if len(r) == 1 or r[1] != '*':
        # The first character in the regex is not succeeded by a *.
        if matches_first_char(s, r):
            return matches(s[1:], r[1:])
        else:
            return False
    else:
        # The first character is succeeded by a *.
        # First, try zero length.
        if matches(s, r[2:]):
            return True

        # If that doesn't match straight away, try globbing more prefixes
        # until the first character of the string doesn't match anymore.
        i = 0
        while matches_first_char(s[i:], r):
            if matches(s[i+1:], r[2:]):
                return True
            i += 1
```

This takes $\mathcal{O}(len(s) \times len(r))$ time and space, since we potentially need to iterate over each suffix substring again for each character.

Fun fact: Stephen Kleene introduced the * operator in regular expressions and as such, it is sometimes referred to as the Kleene star.

12.3 Find array extremes efficiently

Given an array of numbers of length n, find both the minimum and maximum using less than $2*(n-2)$ comparisons.

Solution

It is certainly possible to solve this without using a recursive approach. The trick here is to notice that each comparison actually provides two pieces of information: the smaller element cannot possibly be the maximum of the list, and the larger element cannot be the minimum. So if we take successive pairs of the list, we only need to compare the smaller one to our running minimum, and the larger one to our running maximum.

For example, take the input [4, 2, 7, 5, -1, 3, 6]. To start out, both the minimum and maximum can be initialized as the first element of the list, 4. Then, we examine the next pair to find that 2 is smaller and 7 is bigger. So we update our running minimum to be min(4, 2) = 2 and update our running maximum to be max(4, 7) = 7. Carrying along like this, we would eventually find the minimum and maximum to be -1 and 7, respectively.

Since it takes $n/2$ comparisons to order each pair, and each element will be compared to either the running minimum or maximum, this algorithm uses about $3*n/2$ comparisons.

```
def min_and_max(arr):
    min_element = max_element = arr[0]
    compare = lambda x, y: (x, y) if y > x else (y, x)

    # Make the list odd so we can pair up the remaining elements neatly.
    if len(arr) % 2 == 0:
        arr.append(arr[-1])

    for i in range(1, len(arr), 2):
        smaller, bigger = compare(arr[i], arr[i + 1])
        min_element = min(min_element, smaller)
```

```
        max_element = max(max_element, bigger)

    return min_element, max_element
```

A more elegant approach is to use a technique called divide and conquer. Divide and conquer uses the same base-and-inductive approach as typical recursive solutions, but each subproblem is mutually exclusive. In other words, the input is neatly split into separate divisions which are then combined to form the solution.

For the problem at hand, our base cases are as follows:

- If there is only one element in the array, return that element for both the minimum and maximum.

- If there are two elements, return the smaller one as the minimum, and the larger one as the maximum.

For the general case, we recursively apply our algorithm to the left and right halves of our array, and return the minimum and maximum of the results.

```
def min_and_max(arr):
    if len(arr) == 1:
        return arr[0], arr[0]

    elif len(arr) == 2:
        return (arr[0], arr[1]) if arr[0] < arr[1] else (arr[1], arr[0])

    else:
        n = len(arr) // 2
        lmin, lmax = min_and_max(arr[:n])
        rmin, rmax = min_and_max(arr[n:])
        return min(lmin, rmin), max(lmax, rmax)
```

To be more concrete, here are the intermediate steps when this is applied to the example above:

First, let's recursively break down the array:

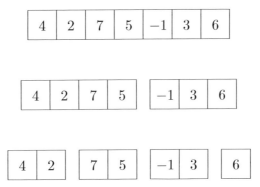

Then, reorder so that smaller comes before larger:

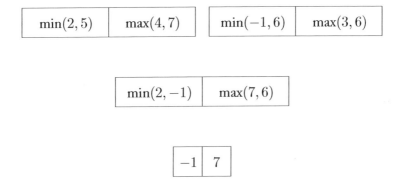

Finally, merge to find min and max:

| min(2, 5) | max(4, 7) | min(−1, 6) | max(3, 6) |

| min(2, −1) | max(7, 6) |

| −1 | 7 |

We can derive the complexity of this algorithm as follows. For each array of size N, we are breaking down the problem into two subproblems of size $n/2$, plus 2 additional comparisons.

More formally, $T(n) = 2 \times T(\frac{n}{2}) + 2$, with base case $T(2) = 1$. When n is a power of two, this recurrence relation resolves exactly to $T(n) = 3 \times \frac{n}{2} - 2$; otherwise, it will take a few more steps.

12.4 Play Nim

The game of Nim is played as follows. Starting with three heaps, each containing a variable number of items, two players take turns removing one or more items from a single pile. The player who eventually is forced to take the last stone loses. For example, if the initial heap sizes are 3, 4, and 5, a game could be played as shown below:

A	B	C	Action
3	4	5	Player 1 takes 3 items from B
3	1	5	Player 2 takes 2 items from C
3	1	3	Player 1 takes 3 items from A
0	1	3	Player 2 takes 3 items from C
0	1	0	Player 1 takes 1 item from A
0	0	0	Player 1 loses

In other words, to start, the first player takes three items from pile B. The second player responds by removing two stones from pile C. The game continues in this way until player one takes the last stone and loses.

Given a list of non-zero starting values [a, b, c], and assuming optimal play, determine whether the first player has a forced win.

Solution

Problems that involve two-player games often can be solved with a minimax approach. Minimax is a recursive algorithm that involves evaluating all possible opponent moves and choosing the one that minimizes the maximum value the opponent can receive.

For the base case, we know that if the piles dwindle down to (0, 0, 0), the current player to move is the winner, since the last player must have removed the final stone.

Now let's say you are faced with the heaps (1, 3, 0). There are many possible moves, but the only good one is to remove everything in pile B, so that your opponent is forced to take the item in pile A. For any other move, there is a response that

CHAPTER 12. RECURSION

makes this a losing game. In other words, the value of a given move to player one is equivalent to the value of the best response to player two.

The list of possible moves can be generated by taking between one and all items from each pile. As a result, we can define a recursive solution that enumerates all possible moves, and returns True if any of them prevent the opponent from making an optimal move.

```python
def update(heaps, pile, items):
    heaps = list(heaps)
    heaps[pile] -= items
    return tuple(heaps)

def get_moves(heaps):
    moves = []

    for pile, count in enumerate(heaps):
        for i in range(1, count + 1):
            moves.append(update(heaps, pile, i))

    return set(moves)

def nim(heaps):
    if heaps == (0, 0, 0):
        return True

    moves = get_moves(heaps)

    return any([nim(move) != True for move in moves])
```

At the start of the game, if each pile has a, b, and c items respectively, there will be $a + b + c$ possible moves, which we can denote by n. Unfortunately, because of our recursive approach, each subsequent move may only bring the number of items down by one, leading to a run time of $\mathcal{O}(n!)$.

In fact, though, there is a bitwise solution to this game that is only $\mathcal{O}(1)$!

Note that the losing state, (0, 0, 0), has an xor product, or "nim-sum", of 0. Though it is trickier to see, it is also the case that for any given state it is possible to make a move that turns this product from zero to non-zero, and vice versa. Therefore, we can use the nim-sum after each pair of moves as an invariant.

More concretely, if you are playing Nim, and for a given move your opponent turns the nim-sum from 0 to 3, you can make a move that turns it back to zero, putting your opponent back in a losing state. As a result, with the exception of one special case, a game is a win for the first player if and only if its nim-sum is nonzero.

```
def nim(heaps):
    a, b, c = heaps
    if a == b == c == 1:
        return False
    
    return a ^ b ^ c != 0
```

13

Dynamic Programming

Dynamic programming is a technique which combines the generality of recursion with the efficiency of greedy algorithms. The key idea is to break a problem down into reusable subproblems which combine to form the solution.

More formally, dynamic programming is an excellent choice when a problem exhibits two key features:

- overlapping subproblems: there is a way to partition the problem into smaller, modular components

- optimal substructure: these modular components can be efficiently put together to obtain a solution

In particular, each subproblem should only be solved once, after which the solution should be cached and reused whenever that state is reached again.

To take a simple example, let's try to figure out the number of ways it is possible to lay pennies and nickels in a line on a table such that they sum to a dollar. If we were solving this with recursion, we might come up with the following recursive relationship:

CHAPTER 13. DYNAMIC PROGRAMMING

```
f(n) = f(n - 5) + f(n - 1)
```

In other words, to get to n we can either add a nickel to a row that previously summed to n - 5, or add a penny to a row that summed to n - 1. Using the base case f(1) = 1, we could solve for n = 100 and eventually compute the answer. Seeing as there are in fact 823, 322, 219, 501 arrangements, this might take a while!

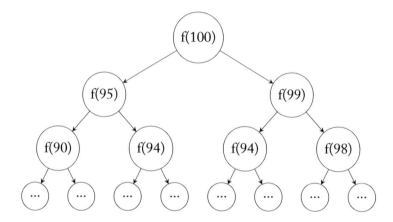

The reason it would take a while is that we are solving the same subproblems over and over again: each computation path is independent, so even though we may have calculated f(50) previously we cannot reuse the result. With dynamic programming, we cache these previous results, so that in effect we perform as many computations as necessary to find the values for f(1), f(2), f(3), and so on, up to f(n).

We have two options for implementing this logic, known as top-down and bottom-up dynamic programming. With the top-down approach, we write code very similar to a recursive solution, but check before each calculation whether the result has already been stored in a cache. This may also be called memoization.

```
def coin_ways(n, cache={0: 1}):
    if n in cache:
        return cache[n]

    if n < 0:
```

CHAPTER 13. DYNAMIC PROGRAMMING

```
        return 0

    cache[n] = coin_ways(n - 1) + coin_ways(n - 5)

    return cache[n]
```

Note how after each call to `coin_ways`, we store the result in our cache.

The bottom-up approach, on the other hand, methodically builds up the values for f(1), f(2), and so on, one after the other, typically by adding values to an array or dictionary. Once all values have been computed, we simply return the final one.

```
def coin_ways(n):
    cache = {0: 1}

    for i in range(1, n + 1):
        cache[i] = cache.get(i - 1, 0) + cache.get(i - 5, 0)

    return cache[n]
```

In general, dynamic programming is a good tool for counting the number of solutions, as in the problem above, or for finding an optimal solution. As such it is frequently used as a building block for more complicated algorithms involving shortest path discovery, text similarity, and combinatorial optimization (such as the knapsack problem).

A method we recommend to solve these problems, and one we will follow in the coming solutions, is to carry out the following steps:

1. Identify the recurrence relation: how can the problem be broken down into smaller parts?

2. Initialize a cache capable of storing the values for each subproblem.

3. Create a memoized function (if top-down) or loop (if bottom-up) which populates these cache values.

CHAPTER 13. DYNAMIC PROGRAMMING

13.1 Number of ways to climb a staircase

There exists a staircase with n steps which you can climb up either 1 or 2 steps at a time. Given n, write a function that returns the number of unique ways you can climb the staircase. The order of the steps matters.

For example, if n is 4, then there are 5 unique ways:

- 1, 1, 1, 1
- 2, 1, 1
- 1, 2, 1
- 1, 1, 2
- 2, 2

Follow-up: what if, instead of being able to climb 1 or 2 steps at a time, you could climb any number from a set of positive integers X? For example, if $X = 1, 3, 5$, you could climb 1, 3, or 5 steps at a time.

Solution

It's always good to start off with some test cases. Let's start with small cases and see if we can find some sort of pattern.

- n = 1: [1]
- n = 2: [1, 1], [2]
- n = 3: [1, 2], [1, 1, 1], [2, 1]
- n = 4: [1, 1, 2], [2, 2], [1, 2, 1], [1, 1, 1, 1], [2, 1, 1]

What's the relationship?

CHAPTER 13. DYNAMIC PROGRAMMING

The only ways to get to $n = 3$ is to first get to $n = 1$ and then go up by 2 steps, or get to $n = 2$ and go up by 1 step. More mathematically, $f(3) = f(2) + f(1)$.

Now let's examine $n = 4$. Here, we can only get to the 4th step by getting to the third step and moving up by one, or by getting to the second step and moving up by two. Therefore, $f(4) = f(3) + f(2)$.

In other words, our recurrence relation is $f(n) = f(n-1) + f(n-2)$. That's just the Fibonacci sequence!

Let's see if we can generalize this to an arbitrary set of steps X. Similar reasoning tells us that if $X = 1, 3, 5$, then our formula should be $f(n) = f(n-1) + f(n-3) + f(n-5)$. If $n < 0$, then we should return 0 since we can't start from a negative number of steps.

```python
def staircase(n, X):
    if n < 0:
        return 0
    elif n == 0:
        return 1
    else:
        return sum(staircase(n - step, X) for step in X)
```

This is still very slow ($\mathcal{O}(|X|^n)$), since we are repeating computations. We can use bottom-up dynamic programming to speed it up.

Each entry `cache[i]` will contain the number of ways we can get to step i with the set X. We will build up the array from zero using the same recurrence as before:

```python
def staircase(n, X):
    cache = [0 for _ in range(n + 1)]
    cache[0] = 1

    for i in range(1, n + 1):
        cache[i] += sum(cache[i - step] for step in X if i - step >= 0)

    return cache[n]
```

CHAPTER 13. DYNAMIC PROGRAMMING

Our algorithm now takes $\mathcal{O}(n \times |X|)$ time and uses $\mathcal{O}(n)$ space, thanks to dynamic programming.

13.2 Number of ways to decode a string

Given the mapping a = 1, b = 2, ..., z = 26, and an encoded message, count the number of ways it can be decoded.

For example, the message "111" should be 3, since it could be decoded as "aaa", "ka", and "ak".

You can assume that the messages are always decodable. For example, "001" is not allowed.

Solution

First, let's try to think of a recurrence we can use for this problem. One way to look for a pattern is to examine some simple cases.

- "", the empty string, should return 1.
- "1" should return 1, since we can parse it as "a" + "".
- "11" should return 2, since we can parse it as "a" + "a" + "" and "k" + "".
- "111" should return 3, since we can parse it as:
    - "a" + "k" + ""
    - "k" + "a" + ""
    - "a" + "a" + "a" + ""
- "011" should return 0, since no letter starts with 0 in our mapping.

This is a good starting point. We can first note that for our base case, any time a string's length is less than or equal to one, there can only be one encoding.

CHAPTER 13. DYNAMIC PROGRAMMING

What happens when the string is at least two digits? There are two possibilities:

- The first letter is encoded alone
- The first two digits form a number k <= 26, and are encoded as a pair

For each of these options, if applicable, we recursively count the number of encodings using the remainder of the string and add them to a running total.

```python
def num_encodings(s, total=0):
    # There is no valid encoding if the string starts with 0.
    if s.startswith('0'):
        return 0

    # Both the empty string and a single character should return 1.
    elif len(s) <= 1:
        return 1

    total += num_encodings(s[1:])

    if int(s[:2]) <= 26:
        total += num_encodings(s[2:])

    return total
```

However, this solution is not very efficient. Every branch calls itself recursively twice, so our runtime is $\mathcal{O}(2^n)$. We can do better by using dynamic programming.

Using an approach typical of bottom-up dynamic programming, we can use the same idea as above, but modify our logic to start from the base case and build up the solution. In particular, we maintain a cache that stores the number of ways to encode any substring s[i:]. Then, for each index from n - 1 down to 0, we compute the number of possible solutions starting at that index and store the result to use in later calculations.

```python
from collections import defaultdict
```

```
def num_encodings(s):
    cache = defaultdict(int)
    cache[len(s)] = 1

    for i in reversed(range(len(s))):
        if s[i].startswith('0'):
            cache[i] = 0
        elif i == len(s) - 1:
            cache[i] = 1
        else:
            cache[i] += cache[i + 1]
            if int(s[i:i + 2]) <= 26:
                cache[i] = cache[i + 2]

    return cache[0]
```

Since each iteration takes $\mathcal{O}(1)$, the whole algorithm now runs in $\mathcal{O}(n) time$.

13.3 Painting houses

A builder is looking to build a row of n houses that can be of k different colors. She has a goal of minimizing cost while ensuring that no two neighboring houses are of the same color.

Given an n by k matrix where the entry at the ith row and j^{th} column represents the cost to build the ith house with the jth color, return the minimum cost required to achieve this goal.

Solution

The brute force solution here would be to generate all possible combinations of houses and colors, filter out invalid combinations, and keep track of the lowest cost seen. This would take $\mathcal{O}(n^k)$ time.

We can solve this problem faster using dynamic programming. We will maintain a matrix cache where every entry [i][j] represents the minimum cost of painting

CHAPTER 13. DYNAMIC PROGRAMMING

house i the color j, as well as painting every house before i. We can calculate this by looking at the minimum cost of painting each house $< i - 1$, and painting house $i - 1$ any color except j, since that would break our constraint. We'll initialize the first row with zeroes to start. Then, we just have to look at the smallest value in the last row of our cache, since that represents the minimum cost of painting every house.

```python
def build_houses(matrix):
    n = len(matrix)
    k = len(matrix[0])
    solution_matrix = [[0] * k]

    # Solution matrix: matrix[i][j] represents the minimum cost to
    # build house i with color j.
    for r, row in enumerate(matrix):
        row_cost = []
        for c, val in enumerate(row):
            row_cost.append(min(solution_matrix[r][i]
                                for i in range(k)
                                if i != c) + val)
        solution_matrix.append(row_cost)

    return min(solution_matrix[-1])
```

This runs in $\mathcal{O}(n \times k^2)$ time and $\mathcal{O}(n \times k)$ space. Can we do even better than this?

First off, notice that we're only ever looking at the last row when computing the next row's cost. That suggests that we only need to keep track of one array of size k instead of a whole matrix of size $n \times k$:

```python
def build_houses(matrix):
    k = len(matrix[0])
    solution_row = [0] * k

    for r, row in enumerate(matrix):
        new_row = []
        for c, val in enumerate(row):
            new_row.append(min(solution_row[i]
```

```
                        for i in range(k)
                        if i != c) + val)
        solution_row = new_row
    return min(solution_row)
```

Now we're only using $\mathcal{O}(k)$ space!

14

Backtracking

Backtracking is an effective technique for solving algorithmic problems. In backtracking, we perform a depth-first search for solutions, jumping back to the last valid path as soon as we hit a dead end.

The benefit of backtracking is that when it is properly implemented, we are guaranteed to find a solution, if one exists. Further, the solution will be more efficient than a brute-force exploration, since we weed out paths that are known to be invalid, a process known as pruning.

On the other hand, backtracking cannot guarantee that we will find an optimal solution, and it often leads to factorial or exponential time complexity if we are required to choose one of M paths at each of N steps.

There are three core questions to ask in order to determine whether backtracking is the right algorithm to use for a problem.

1. Can you construct a partial solution?
2. Can you verify if the partial solution is invalid?
3. Can you verify if the solution is complete?

To illustrate this concept, we will walk through one of the most common example of backtracking: the N queens puzzle. In this problem, you are given an `N x N` board, and asked to find the number of ways N queens can be placed on the board without threatening each other. More explicitly, no two queens are allowed to share the same row, column, or diagonal.

- Can we construct a partial solution?

Yes, we can tentatively place queens on the board.

- Can we verify if the partial solution is invalid?

Yes, we can check a solution is invalid if two queens threaten each other. To speed this up, we can assume that all queens already placed so far do not threaten each other, so we only need to check if the last queen we added attacks any other queen.

- Can we verify if the solution is complete?

Yes, we know a solution is complete if all N queens have been placed.

Now that we are confident that we can use backtracking, let's implement it. We'll loop through the first row and try placing a queen in each column from left to right. If we are able to find a valid location, we continue with the second row, and third row, and so on, up to N. What differs here from brute force is that we'll be adding the queens incrementally instead of all at once.

We will create an `is_valid` function that checks the board on each incremental addition. This function will look at the last queen placed and see if any other queen can threaten it. If so, we prune the branch, since there's no point pursuing it. Otherwise, we'll recursively call our function with the new incremental solution. We only stop once we hit the base case, which is when we've placed all queens on the board already.

We can represent our board as a one-dimensional array of integers from 1 to n, where the value at index i represents the column the queen on row i is on. Since we're working incrementally, we don't even need to initialize the whole board. We can just append and pop as we go down the stack.

Here's the actual code in Python:

```python
def n_queens(n, board=[]):
    if n == len(board):
        return 1

    count = 0
    for col in range(n):
        board.append(col)
        if is_valid(board):
            count += n_queens(n, board)
        board.pop()
    return count

def is_valid(board):
    current_queen_row, current_queen_col = len(board) - 1, board[-1]

    # Check if any queens can attack the last queen.
    for row, col in enumerate(board[:-1]):
        diff = abs(current_queen_col - col)
        if diff == 0 or diff == current_queen_row - row:
            return False
    return True
```

Now that you've got the hang of it, try your hand at some more interesting problems.

14.1 Compute flight itinerary

Given an unordered list of flights taken by someone, each represented as (origin, destination) pairs, and a starting airport, compute a possible itinerary. If no such itinerary exists, return null. All flights must be used in the itinerary.

For example, given the list of flights [('SFO', 'HKO'), ('YYZ', 'SFO'), ('YUL', 'YYZ'), ('HKO', 'ORD')] and starting airport 'YUL', you may return the list ['YUL',

'YYZ', 'SFO', 'HKO', 'ORD'].

Given the list of flights [('SFO', 'COM'), ('COM', 'YYZ')] and starting airport 'COM', you should return null.

Solution

Let's walk through our three-step process.

- Can we construct a partial solution?

Yes, we can build an (incomplete) itinerary and extend it by adding more flights to the end.

- Can we verify if the partial solution is invalid?

Yes, a solution is invalid if there are no flights leaving from our last destination, and there are still flights remaining that can be taken. Since we must use all flights, this would mean we are at a dead end.

- Can we verify if the solution is complete?

Yes, we can check if a solution is complete if our itinerary uses all the flights.

Our strategy then will be as follows. We maintain a list that represents the current itinerary. For each possible next flight, we try appending it to our path, and call our function recursively on this new itinerary with the leftover flights. If no path can succeed, we pop the last addition and continue.

```python
def get_itinerary(flights, current_itinerary):
    # If we've used up all the flights, we're done
    if not flights:
        return current_itinerary
```

CHAPTER 14. BACKTRACKING

```
        last_stop = current_itinerary[-1]
        for i, (origin, destination) in enumerate(flights):
            # Make a copy of flights without the current one to mark it as
            # used
            flights_minus_current = flights[:i] + flights[i + 1:]
            current_itinerary.append(destination)
            if origin == last_stop:
                return get_itinerary(flights_minus_current, current_itinerary)
            current_itinerary.pop()

        return None
```

At each step i, there will be i - 1 continuation paths to explore. As a result, similar to the preceding n-queens problem, our time and space complexity will be $\mathcal{O}(n!)$ in the worst case.

14.2 Solve Sudoku

Sudoku is a puzzle where you're given a 9 by 9 grid partially filled with digits. The objective is to fill the grid subject to the constraint that every row, column, and box (3 by 3 subgrid) must contain all of the digits from 1 to 9.

Here is an example sudoku puzzle:

2	5			3		9		1
	1				4			
4		7				2		8
		5	2					
				9	8	1		
	4				3			
				3	6		7	2
	7							3
9		3				6		4

And this is its solution:

2	5	8	7	3	6	9	4	1
6	1	9	8	2	4	3	5	7
4	3	7	9	1	5	2	6	8
3	9	5	2	7	1	4	8	6
7	6	2	4	9	8	1	3	5
8	4	1	6	5	3	7	2	9
1	8	4	3	6	9	5	7	2
5	7	6	1	4	2	8	9	3
9	2	3	5	8	7	6	1	4

Implement an efficient sudoku solver.

Solution

Trying brute force on a sudoku board will take a really long time: we will need to try every permutation of the numbers $1-9$ for all the non-empty squares.

Let's try using backtracking to solve this problem instead. We can fill each empty cell one by one and backtrack once we hit an invalid state.

By now you should know the drill.

- Can we construct a partial solution?

Yes, we can fill in some portions of the board.

- Can we verify if the partial solution is invalid?

Yes, we can check that the board is valid so far if there are no rows, columns, or squares that contain the same digit.

- Can we verify if the solution is complete?

CHAPTER 14. BACKTRACKING

Yes, the solution is complete when the board has been filled up.

For our algorithm, we will try filling each empty cell one by one, and backtrack once we hit an invalid state.

To do this, we'll need a `valid_so_far` function that tests the board for its validity by checking all the rows, columns, and squares. Then we'll backtrack as usual:

```
EMPTY = 0

def sudoku(board):
    if is_complete(board):
        return board

    # Set r, c to values from 1 to 9.
    r, c = find_first_empty(board)

    for i in range(1, 10):
        board[r][c] = i
        if valid_so_far(board):
            result = sudoku(board)
            if is_complete(result):
                return result
        board[r][c] = EMPTY
    return board

def is_complete(board):
    return all(all(val is not EMPTY for val in row) for row in board)

def find_first_empty(board):
    for i, row in enumerate(board):
        for j, val in enumerate(row):
            if val == EMPTY:
                return i, j
    return False

def valid_so_far(board):
    if not rows_valid(board):
        return False
    if not cols_valid(board):
        return False
    if not blocks_valid(board):
```

```
            return False
    return True

def rows_valid(board):
    for row in board:
        if duplicates(row):
            return False
    return True

def cols_valid(board):
    for j in range(len(board[0])):
        if duplicates([board[i][j] for i in range(len(board))]):
            return False
    return True

def blocks_valid(board):
    for i in range(0, 9, 3):
        for j in range(0, 9, 3):
            block = []
            for k in range(3):
                for l in range(3):
                    block.append(board[i + k][j + l])
            if duplicates(block):
                return False
    return True

def duplicates(arr):
    c = {}
    for val in arr:
        if val in c and val is not EMPTY:
            return True
        c[val] = True
    return False
```

14.3 Count Android unlock combinations

One way to unlock an Android phone is by swiping in a specific pattern across a $1-9$ keypad, which looks like this:

CHAPTER 14. BACKTRACKING

1	2	3
4	5	6
7	8	9

For a pattern to be valid, it must satisfy the following criteria:

- All of its keys must be distinct.

- It must not connect two keys by jumping over a third key, unless that key has already been used.

For example, 4 - 2 - 1 - 7 is a valid pattern, whereas 2 - 1 - 7 is not.

Find the total number of valid unlock patterns of length n, where 1 <= n <= 9.

Solution

Let's first try to solve the problem without any restrictions on jumping over keys. If there are n starting numbers to choose from, we will have $n - 1$ options for the second number, $n - 2$ options for the third, and so on.

Each time we visit a number, we mark it as visited, traverse all paths starting with that number, and then remove it from the visited set. Along the way we keep a running count of the number of paths seen thus far, which we eventually return as our result.

```
def num_paths(current, visited, n):
    if n == 1:
        return 1

    paths = 0
    for number in range(1, 10):
        if number not in visited:
```

CHAPTER 14. BACKTRACKING

```
            visited.add(number)
            paths += num_paths(number, jumps, visited, n - 1)
            visited.remove(number)

    return paths
```

To modify this to account for jumps, we can use a dictionary mapping pairs of keys to the key they skip over. Before visiting a number, we check to see that either the current and next number do not exist as a pair in this dictionary, or that their value has already been visited.

Notice also that because of the symmetry of the keypad, the number of patterns starting from 1 is the same as the number of patterns starting from 3, 7, and 9. For example, the path $1 - 6 - 3 - 8$ can be rotated 180 degrees to get $9 - 4 - 7 - 2$. Similarly, paths starting with 2, 4, 6, and 8 are all rotationally symmetric. As a result, our answer can be expressed as `4 * num_paths(1) + 4 * num_paths(2) + 1 * num_paths(5)`.

Putting it all together, the solution should look something like this:

```
def num_paths(current, jumps, visited, n):
    if n == 1:
        return 1

    paths = 0
    for number in range(1, 10):
        if number not in visited:
            if (current, number) not in jumps or \
            jumps[(current, number)] in visited:
                visited.add(number)
                paths += num_paths(number, jumps, visited, n - 1)
                visited.remove(number)

    return paths

def unlock_combinations(n):
    jumps = {(1, 3): 2, (1, 7): 4, (1, 9): 5,
             (2, 8): 5,
             (3, 1): 2, (3, 7): 5, (3, 9): 6,
```

```
                (4, 6): 5, (6, 4): 5,
                (7, 1): 4, (7, 3): 5, (7, 9): 8,
                (8, 2): 5,
                (9, 1): 5, (9, 3): 6, (9, 7): 8}

    return 4 * num_paths(1, jumps, set([1]), n) + \
           4 * num_paths(2, jumps, set([2]), n) + \
           1 * num_paths(5, jumps, set([5]), n)
```

Even though the jump restrictions have limited the options at each next step, the time complexity for each of the three starting points is still $\mathcal{O}(n!)$.

15

Sorting and Searching

Given the fundamental importance of arrays, it is only natural that computer scientists have developed many tools for finding and ordering their elements.

You may be familiar with classic sorting methods like quicksort and mergesort. Both are comparison sorting algorithms that use a divide-and-conquer technique. In quicksort, we choose a pivot element, move other elements to the left or right of this element depending on if they are smaller or larger, and then recursively sort the elements on either side. It has a worst-case performance of $\mathcal{O}(n^2)$, but on average takes $\mathcal{O}(n \log n)$. For merge sort, we repeatedly divide our array into subarrays and then join them so that larger and larger pieces end up sorted.

While it is worth implementing these from scratch on your own time, in an interview setting it is more likely that you can rely on your preferred language's built-in `sort` functionality for this purpose. Instead, this chapter will focus on how to recognize the importance of sorting in a given problem, and when and how to apply more specific sorting algorithms.

If an array is already sorted, you should leap to binary search as a potential solution. Instead of having to traverse each element, binary search cuts the search time down to $\mathcal{O}(\log n)$, where n is the length of the array.

Binary search works by cutting down the search space in half, adjusting either the

CHAPTER 15. SORTING AND SEARCHING

left or right bound and recursively looking in the new subarray. For example, suppose we have the ten-element array [4, 5, 6, 15, 29, 65, 88, 99, 190, 250, 300], and we are seeking the element 15. We can achieve this in only three steps:

- First, we compare 15 to the element at index 5. Since 15 < 65, we shift our upper bound index down to 4. Our search space is now [4, 5, 6, 15, 29].

- Next, we compare 15 to the element at index 2. Since 15 > 6, we shift our lower bound index up to 3. Our search space is now [15, 29].

- Finally, we compare 15 to the element at index 3, and find what we are looking for.

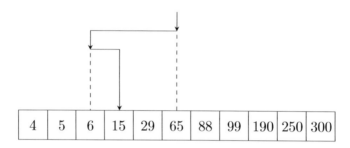

We can code this iteratively or recursively; here is how an iterative version would look:

```
def binary_search(array, x):
    low = 0; high = len(array) - 1
    found = False

    while low <= high and not found:
        mid = (low + high) // 2

        if x == array[mid]:
            found = True
        elif x < array[mid]:
            high = mid - 1
        else:
            low = mid + 1
```

```
    return found
```

Implementing binary search can frequently be tricky, due to subtle off-by-one index errors. As a result, it is not a bad idea to become familiar with a built-in library that can perform this task for you, such as Python's `bisect` module.

Let's now apply these ideas to a few problems.

15.1 Dutch flag problem

Given an array of strictly the characters R, G, and B, segregate the values of the array so that all the Rs come first, the Gs come second, and the Bs come last. You can only swap elements of the array.

Do this in linear time and in-place.

For example, given the array `['G', 'B', 'R', 'R', 'B', 'R', 'G']`, you should transform it to `['R', 'R', 'R', 'G', 'G', 'B', 'B']`.

Solution

Let's first consider an easier problem, where there are only the two values R and G. In this case, we can think of our array as being split into three sections. Regardless of what happens, we will try to maintain the loop invariant that only Rs will be in the first section, only Gs will be in the third section, and unidentified elements will remain in the middle section.

If we let `low` and `high` be the indices marking the section boundaries, we can represent these areas as follows:

- Strictly Rs: `array[:low]`

- Unknown: `array[low:high]`

- Strictly *G*s: `array[high:]`

Initially, `low` and `high` will be set to the first and last elements of the array, respectively, since every element is unknown. As we iterate over the array, we will swap any *G*s we see to the third section and decrement `high`. Meanwhile, whenever we see an *R*, we will increment `low`, since the boundary of red characters must shift forward. In this way, we gradually shrink the unknown section down to nothing, finally terminating our algorithm once the two indices meet.

```python
def partition(arr):
    low, high = 0, len(arr) - 1
    while low <= high:
        if arr[low] == 'R':
            low += 1
        else:
            arr[low], arr[high] = arr[high], arr[low]
            high -= 1
```

This correctly splits our array into two separate categories. How can we extend this to three partitions?

Using a similar idea to the method above, we can maintain four sections using 3 indices: `low`, `mid`, and `high`. The contents of each section will be as follows:

- Strictly *R*s: `array[:low]`

- Strictly *G*s: `array[low:mid]`

- Unknown: `array[mid:high]`

- Strictly *B*s: `array[high:]`

As before, we will initialize `low` and `high` to be the first and last elements of our array, respectively. Additionally, `mid` will initially be equal to `low`. The key to this strategy is that we will keep incrementing our midpoint index and moving the corresponding element to the appropriate location.

CHAPTER 15. SORTING AND SEARCHING

More concretely:

- If the element is R, we swap `array[mid]` with `array[low]` and increment `low`.

- If the element is G, we do nothing, since this element belongs in the middle.

- If the element is B, we swap `array[mid]` with `array[high]` and decrement `high`.

When our `mid` and `high` indices meet, we know that the unknown section is gone and we can terminate our algorithm.

```python
def partition(arr):
    low, mid, high = 0, 0, len(arr) - 1
    while mid <= high:
        if arr[mid] == 'R':
            arr[low], arr[mid] = arr[mid], arr[low]
            low += 1
            mid += 1
        elif arr[mid] == 'G':
            mid += 1
        else:
            arr[mid], arr[high] = arr[high], arr[mid]
            high -= 1
```

P.S. This problem is also called the Dutch national flag problem, since that flag consists of three horizontal stripes of red, white and blue.

15.2 Pancake sort

Given a list, sort it using the helper method `reverse(lst, i, j)`.

This method takes a sublist as indicated by the left and right bounds `i` and `j` and reverses all its elements. For example, `reverse([10, 20, 30, 40, 50], 1, 3)` would result in `[10, 40, 30, 20, 50]`.

Solution

This type of sorting is also called pancake sorting, since the process of reversing sublists is analogous to flipping a pancake. We can approach this problem using a technique similar to selection sort. The idea is to iteratively place the maximum remaining element at the end of the list.

To see how this works, let `size` be the size of the list that we're concerned with sorting at the moment. We can iterate over the first `size` elements of the list to find the position of the maximum element, say `max_ind`. In order to place this element at the end, we perform two steps:

- Reverse the sublist from 0 to `max_ind` to move the max element to the front.
- Then, reverse the sublist from 0 to `size` to move the max element to the end.

Finally, we decrement `size` and repeat, until there is nothing left to sort.

```python
def pancake_sort(lst):
    for size in reversed(range(len(lst))):
        max_ind = max_pos(lst[:size + 1])
        reverse(lst, 0, max_ind)
        reverse(lst, 0, size)

    return lst

def max_pos(lst):
    return lst.index(max(lst))

def reverse(lst, i, j):
    while i < j:
        lst[i], lst[j] = lst[j], lst[i]
        i += 1
        j -= 1
```

This algorithm takes $\mathcal{O}(n^2)$ time and $\mathcal{O}(1)$ space.

15.3 Efficiently sort a billion integers

Given an array of a million integers between zero and a billion, out of order, how would you efficiently sort it? Assume that you cannot store an array of a billion elements in memory.

Solution

Sorting by an algorithm like quicksort or merge sort would give us an average time complexity of $\mathcal{O}(n \log n)$. But we can take advantage of the fact that our input is bounded and only consists of integers to do even better. One algorithm that performs particularly well in these cases is called radix sort.

To see how this works, suppose we have a list of non-negative numbers, such as [4, 100, 54, 537, 2, 89], and we know ahead of time that no number has more than three digits. Then we can (stably) sort our list using three passes, corresponding to each digit:

- First, we order by the ones' place, giving us [100, 2, 4, 54, 537, 89].
- Next, we order by the tens' place, giving us [100, 2, 4, 537, 54, 89].
- Finally, we order by the hundreds' place, giving us [2, 4, 54, 89, 100, 537].

Note that if a given number doesn't have a tens' or hundreds' place, we assign that place value zero.

Each of these sorts is performed using counting sort, which gets around the efficiency limits of comparison sorts like quicksort. In counting sort, we assign each number to a bucket, and store each bucket as an element in an array of size equal to our base, in this case 10. Then, we read off the elements in each bucket, in order, to get the new sorted array.

We can implement this as follows:

```
def counting_sort(array, digit, base=10):
    counts = [[] for _ in range(base)]

    for num in array:
        d = (num // base ** digit) % base
        counts[d].append(num)

    result = []
    for bucket in counts:
        result.extend(bucket)

    return result

def radix_sort(array, digits=10):
    for digit in range(digits):
        array = counting_sort(array, digit)

    return array
```

Counting sort takes $\mathcal{O}(n + m)$, where n is the length of our input and m is the number of buckets. Since $m \ll n$, we can consider this to be $\mathcal{O}(n)$. We must perform this sort once for each digit in the largest integer. If the largest integer has k digits, the time complexity of this algorithm will be $\mathcal{O}(n * k)$.

15.4 Find minimum element in rotated sorted array

A sorted array of integers has been rotated an unknown number of times.

Given this array, find the index of an element in the array in faster than linear time. If the element doesn't exist in the array, return null.

For example, given the array `[13, 18, 25, 2, 8, 10]` and the element 8, return 4 (the index of 8 in the array).

You can assume all the integers in the array are unique.

Solution

We can obviously do this problem in linear time if we iterate over the array and examine each element. How can we make this more efficient?

Whenever there is extra information given in an interview question, it pays to think about how it can be used. In this case, a big clue should be that the array of integers was previously sorted and then rotated. As we mention in the introduction, binary search is an excellent technique for finding elements that are sorted. However, we must make some tweaks to apply this to our rotated array.

In our solution, we first find the rotation point using binary search. Initially, our `low` and `high` indices will be the start and end of our array. At each step we compare the midpoint of our array to the first element, and make the following updates:

- If the midpoint is larger, the pivot must come after it, so we set `low` to be the midpoint.
- If the midpoint is smaller, the pivot must come before it, so we set `high` to be the midpoint.

With each iteration, we cut the search space in half in order to find the index at which the original list was rotated.

Once we have this rotation point, we can do binary search as usual by remembering to offset by the correct amount.

The code would look like this:

```python
def shifted_array_search(lst, num):
    # First, find where the breaking point is in the shifted array.
    i = len(lst) // 2
    dist = i // 2
    while True:
        if lst[0] > lst[i] and lst[i - 1] > lst[i]:
            break
        elif dist == 0:
            break
```

```
        elif lst[0] <= lst[i]:
            i = i + dist
        elif lst[i - 1] <= lst[i]:
            i = i - dist
        else:
            break
        dist = dist // 2

    # Now that we have the bottom, we can do binary search as usual,
    # wrapping around the rotation.
    low = i
    high = i - 1
    dist = len(lst) // 2
    while True:
        if dist == 0:
            return None

        guess_ind = (low + dist) % len(lst)
        guess = lst[guess_ind]

        if guess == num:
            return guess_ind
        if guess < num:
            low = (low + dist) % len(lst)
        if guess > num:
            high = (len(lst) + high - dist) % len(lst)

        dist = dist // 2
```

This solution runs in $\mathcal{O}(\log n)$. However, this is definitely not the only solution! There are many other possible ways to implement this, but as long as you have the idea of doing binary search, you've got it.

16

Pathfinding

Since graphs can be used to represent almost anything, computer scientists have spent a lot of time and energy trying to find efficient algorithms for manipulating them.

One particularly rich area of application is that of pathfinding. The goal of these algorithms is to find the shortest, least expensive, or otherwise best path through a graph with weighted edges. Whether it is powering GPS systems, modeling the spread of diseases, or calculating the best route through a maze containing hidden treasure, pathfinding algorithms frequently come in handy.

In particular, in this chapter we will focus on three important algorithms. First, we motivate and explain Dijkstra's algorithm, used to find the shortest path from one node to all other nodes. Next, we take a look at Bellman-Ford, which is similar to Dijkstra's algorithm except it can also handle negative edge weights. Finally, we explore the Floyd-Warshall algorithm, which efficiently finds the shortest path between every pair of nodes in a graph.

CHAPTER 16. PATHFINDING

16.1 Dijkstra's algorithm

A network consists of nodes labeled 0 to n. You are given a list of edges (a, b, t), describing the time t in seconds it takes for a message to be sent from node a to node b. Whenever a node receives a message, it immediately passes the message on to a neighboring node, if possible.

Assuming all nodes are connected, determine how long it will take for every node to receive a message that begins at node 0.

For example, given $n = 5$ and the following graph:

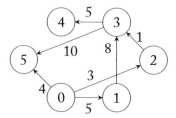

You should return 9, because propagating the message from `0 -> 2 -> 3 -> 4` will take nine seconds.

For convenience, here is the list of weighted edges (`u`, `v`, `weight`) for this graph.

```
[
    (0, 1, 5),
    (0, 2, 3),
    (0, 5, 4),
    (1, 3, 8),
    (2, 3, 1),
    (3, 5, 10),
    (3, 4, 5)
]
```

Solution

To help organize our input, we can think of the network nodes as vertices on a graph, and each connection as an edge. We will use a helper class that maps each node to a list of tuples of the form (`neighbor, time`).

```
class Network:
    def __init__(self, N, edges):
        self.vertices = range(N + 1)
        self.edges = edges

    def make_graph(self):
        graph = {v: [] for v in network.vertices}

        for u, v, w in network.edges:
            graph[u].append((v, w))

        return graph
```

Finding the shortest amount of time it will take for each node to receive the message, then, is equivalent to finding the shortest path between vertex 0 and all other vertices. For this we can use Dijkstra's algorithm.

Put briefly, Dijkstra's algorithm is used to compute the shortest path between two vertices of a graph, under the assumption that all edges have nonnegative weight. It works by repeatedly traveling to the closest vertex which has not yet been reached.

We will first create a dictionary, `times`, mapping each node to the minimum amount of time it takes for a message to propagate to it. Initially this will be infinite for all nodes except the start node, which is zero.

Then, we consider an unvisited node with the smallest propagation time. For each of its neighbors, we replace the propagation time for that neighbor with the time it would take to go through the current node to get to that neighbor, if the latter is smaller. We continue this process until we have visited all nodes.

In the end, the largest value in our dictionary will represent the time it will take for the last node to get the message.

```
def propagate(network):
    graph = network.make_graph()
    times = {node: float('inf') for node in graph}
    times[0] = 0

    q = list(graph)
    while q:
        u = min(q, key=lambda x: times[x])
        q.remove(u)
        for v, time in graph[u]:
            times[v] = min(times[v], times[u] + time)

    return max(times.values())
```

Since we must find the minimum value of our dictionary for each unexamined node, and there are n nodes, this will take $\mathcal{O}(n^2)$ time.

For sparse graphs, we can improve on this by using a priority queue, ordering each node by propagation time. To start, this queue will just hold node zero, with value zero.

Starting from 0, then, each time we encounter a new neighbor, we add it to the queue, with value equal to the sum of the time from node zero to the current node, and from the current node to the neighbor. Whenever we pop a node off the queue that does not exist in our `times` dictionary, we add a new key with the corresponding value.

```
def propagate(network):
    graph = network.make_graph()
    times = {}

    q = [(0, 0)]
    while q:
        u, node = heapq.heappop(q)
        if node not in times:
```

CHAPTER 16. PATHFINDING

```
            times[node] = u
        for neighbor, v in graph[node]:
            if neighbor not in times:
                heapq.heappush(q, (u + v, neighbor))

    return max(times.values())
```

It takes $\mathcal{O}(\log E)$ time to pop or push an element from the heap, and we must do this for each edge, so the complexity of this algorithm is $\mathcal{O}(E \log E)$.

16.2 Bellman-Ford

Given a table of currency exchange rates, represented as a 2-D array, determine whether there is a possible arbitrage opportunity. That is, find out if there is some sequence of trades you can make, starting with some amount X of any currency, so that you can end up with some amount greater than X of that currency.

Here is one possible sample input, describing the exchange rates between the US dollar, the pound sterling, the Indian rupee, and the euro.

```
graph = {
    'USD' : {'GBP': 0.77, 'INR': 71.71, 'EUR': 0.87},
    'GBP' : {'USD': 1.30, 'INR': 93.55, 'EUR': 1.14},
    'INR' : {'USD': 0.014, 'GBP': 0.011, 'EUR': 0.012},
    'EUR' : {'USD': 1.14, 'GBP': 0.88, 'INR': 81.95}
}
```

Assume that there are no transaction costs and you can trade fractional quantities.

Solution

For this question, we can model the currencies and exchange rates as a graph, where nodes are currencies and edges are the exchange rates between each currency. We can assume that our table contains rates for every possible pair of currencies, so that the graph is complete. To solve this problem, then, we must determine if it is possible to find a cycle whose edge weight product is greater than 1.

Unfortunately, all the algorithms we described in the introduction deal with computing the sum of edge weights, not the product! However, with a little math we can fix this issue.

Recall that one of the properties of logarithms is that $\log(a \times b) = \log(a) + \log(b)$. Therefore, if we take the logarithm of each exchange rate, and negate it to ensure that weights are positive, we can transform this problem into one of finding a negative sum cycle. And luckily for us, we can use the Bellman-Ford algorithm for just this purpose.

As a refresher, the Bellman-Ford algorithm is commonly used to find the shortest path between a source vertex and each of the other vertices. If the graph contains a negative cycle, however, it can detect it and throw an exception (or, in our case, return true).

The Bellman-Ford algorithms works as follows. We begin by fixing a source node, and setting the distance to all other nodes to infinity. Then, for each edge (u, v) in our graph, we check if it is more efficient to get to v along the edge from u than the current best option. If so, we update the distance value for v.

Note that for any graph with V vertices, the longest path can have at most $|V| - 1$ edges. As a result, we can repeat the above operation $|V| - 1$ times and eventually arrive at the optimal way to reach each vertex.

If after $|V| - 1$ iterations, we can still find a smaller path, there must be a negative cycle in the graph.

```python
from math import log

def arbitrage(table):
    transformed_graph = [[-log(edge) for edge in row] for row in graph]

    # Pick any source vertex - we can run Bellman-Ford from any vertex and
    # get the right result
```

```
        source = 0
        n = len(transformed_graph)
        min_dist = [float('inf')] * n

        min_dist[source] = 0

        # Relax edges |V - 1| times
        for i in range(n - 1):
            for v in range(n):
                for w in range(n):
                    if min_dist[w] > min_dist[v] + transformed_graph[v][w]:
                        min_dist[w] = min_dist[v] + transformed_graph[v][w]

        # If we can still relax edges, then we have a negative cycle
        for v in range(n):
            for w in range(n):
                if min_dist[w] > min_dist[v] + transformed_graph[v][w]:
                    return True

        return False
```

Because of the triply-nested for loop, this runs in $\mathcal{O}(N^3)$ time.

16.3 Floyd-Warshall

The transitive closure of a graph is a measure of which vertices are reachable from other vertices. It can be represented as a matrix M, where `M[i][j] == 1` if there is a path between vertices i and j, and otherwise 0.

For example, suppose we are given the following graph:

The transitive closure of this graph would be:

```
[1, 1, 1, 1]
[0, 1, 1, 0]
[0, 0, 1, 0]
[0, 0, 0, 1]
```

Given a graph, find its transitive closure.

Solution

One algorithm we can use to solve this is a modified version of Floyd-Warshall.

Traditionally Floyd-Warshall is used for finding the shortest path between all vertices in a weighted graph. It works in the following way: for any pair of nodes (i, j), we check to see if there is an intermediate vertex k such that the cost of getting from i to k to j is less than the current cost of getting from i to j. This is generalized by examining each possible choice of k, and updating every (i, j) cost that can be improved.

In our case, we are concerned not with costs but simply with whether it is possible to get from i to j. So we can start with a boolean matrix reachable filled with zeros, except for the connections given in our adjacency matrix.

Then, for each intermediate node k, and for each connection (i, j), if reachable[i][j] is zero but there is a path from i to k and from k to j, we should change it to one.

```python
def closure(graph):
    n = len(graph)
    reachable = [[0 for _ in range(n)] for _ in range(n)]

    for i, v in enumerate(graph):
        for neighbor in v:
            reachable[i][neighbor] = 1

    for k in range(n):
        for i in range(n):
            for j in range(n):
```

```
                    reachable[i][j] |= (reachable[i][k] and reachable[k][j])

    return reachable
```

Since we are looping through three levels of vertices, this will take $\mathcal{O}(V^3)$ time. Our matrix uses $\mathcal{O}(V^2)$ space.

17

Bit Manipulation

Questions on bit manipulation questions are the curveballs of coding interviews: they're less common, and can frequently trip up candidates who are unprepared. But as we will explore below, as long as you understand a few key concepts you'll find these problems are actually very approachable.

First, let's discuss what a bit is. A bit, short for binary digit, is either 0 or 1. String a bunch of these bits together, and you can represent any integer. Each place value, starting from the right column and extending left, represents a power of two, so that 00000101 stands for 5 ($2^0 + 2^2$). In this example we've represented 5 as an 8-bit number, and most of the bits are zero, or "off".

To negate an n-bit number, we use an operation called **two's complement**, which is to say we invert all the bits and then add one. As a result, 5 would become 11111011.

Bits are useful because they provide an extremely fast and space-efficient way of calculating numerical operations. In particular, you should be familiar with the following three operators:

- & (AND)

The bitwise AND takes two integers as input and produces a third integer whose bits are 1 if and only if both corresponding input bits are 1.

For example, `00000101 & 00011110 = 00000100`.

- | (OR)

The bitwise OR takes two integers as input and produces a third integer whose bits are 1 if either corresponding input bit is 1.

For example, `00000101 | 00011110 = 00011111`.

- ^ (XOR)

The bitwise XOR takes two integers as input and produces a third integer whose bits are 1 if the corresponding input bits are different. That is, for each place one of the input integers must be 0 and the other must be 1.

For example, `00000101 ^ 00011110 = 00011011`.

Bits also provide a quick way of multiplying or dividing a number by powers of two. This method is called **bitshifting**, and is represented by the symbols << and >>. In effect, << inserts zeroes at the right end of the bit, so that each corresponding bit is shifted to the left. Conversely, >> can be thought of as inserting zeroes at the left end of the bit, pushing elements rightward.

Here are some bitshifts in action:

`5 << 2 = 20 (00000101 << 2 = 00010100)`

`5 >> 2 = 1 (00000101 >> 2 = 00000001)`

Note that in the last example, when we "push" the last two bits to the right, they essentially disappear.

Some common questions that you can expect in this topic are clearing and setting bits, reversing bits, and using a bit representation to more efficiently solve problems that can be translated into binary.

Let's dive in.

Chapter 17. Bit Manipulation

17.1 Find element that appears once in list

Given an array of integers where every integer occurs three times except for one integer, which only occurs once, find and return the non-duplicated integer.

For example, given [6, 1, 3, 3, 3, 6, 6], return 1. Given [13, 19, 13, 13], return 19.

Do this in $\mathcal{O}(N)$ time and $\mathcal{O}(1)$ space.

Solution

We can find the unique number in an array of two duplicates by XORing all the numbers in the array. What this does is cancel out all the bits that have an even number of 1s, leaving only the unique (odd) bits out.

Let's try to extend this technique to three duplicates. Instead of cancelling out all the bits with an even number of ones, we want to cancel those with a multiple of three.

Let's assume all integers fit in 32 bits. First, we will create an array 32 zeroes long. When iterating over each number in our array, we can match up each bit to its proper spot in this array and increment a counter if that bit is set. Finally, we'll go over each bit in the array, and if the value at that index is not a multiple of three, we know to include that bit in our result.

```python
def find_unique(arr):
    result_arr = [0] * 32
    for num in arr:
        for i in range(32):
            bit = num >> i & 1
            result_arr[i] += bit

    result = 0
    for i, bit in enumerate(result_arr):
        if bit % 3 != 0:
            result += 2 ** i
```

```
            return result
```

This runs in linear time, since we iterate over the array once, and in constant space, since we initialize an array of constant size.

17.2 Implement division without / or * operators

Implement division of two positive integers without using the division, multiplication, or modulus operators. Return the quotient as an integer, ignoring the remainder.

Solution

We can start by trying the simplest solution. Define x as the dividend and y as the divisor. To get the quotient, we need to ask how many times we can subtract y from x until the remainder is less than y. The number of times we subtract is the resulting quotient $\frac{x}{y}$. The time complexity of this brute force approach is on the order of $\frac{x}{y}$, which can be very high, for example if x is $2^{31} - 1$ and y is 1.

Let's instead think about how to perform division on paper. Recall grade-school long division, where we consider the left-most digit that can be divided by the divisor. At each step, the quotient becomes the first digit of the result, and we subtract the product from the dividend to get the remainder. The remainder is initially the value x. We can abstract this process into subtracting the largest multiple of $y \times 10^d$ from the remainder, where d is the place of the digit ($d = 0$ for the zeros place). Then we add the multiple times 10^d to our result.

This process would be straightforward if we had the modulus or multiplication operators. However, we instead can take advantage of the bit shift operators in order to multiply by powers of two, since a << z results in a multiplied by 2^z (e.g. 3 << 2 = 12). Now, we can find the largest $y \times 2^d$ that fits within the remainder. As we do in long division, we decrease the possible value of d in each iteration. We start by finding the largest value of $y \times 2^d \leq x$, then test $y \times 2^d, y \times 2^{d-1}, \ldots$, until the remainder is less than y.

For example, let's say we want to divide x = 31 by y = 3. Here are the steps we'd follow:

Step	x (binary)	Quotient (decimal)
Start	11111	0
$y \times 2^3$ fits in x	11111 - (11 « 3) = 0111	1 « 3
$y \times 2^1$ fits in x	111 - (11 « 1) = 1	(1 « 3) + (1 « 1) = **10**

Here is the Python implementation:

```python
def divide(x, y):
    if y == 0:
        raise ZeroDivisionError('Division by zero')

    quotient = 0
    power = 32              # Assume 32-bit integer
    y_power = y << power    # Initial y^d value is y^32
    remainder = x           # Initial remainder is x
    while remainder >= y:
        while y_power > remainder:
            y_power >>= 1
            power -= 1
        quotient += 1 << power
        remainder -= y_power

    return quotient
```

The time complexity of this solution is $\mathcal{O}(n)$, where n is the number of bits used to represent x/y, assuming shift and add operations take $\mathcal{O}(1)$ time.

17.3 Compute longest consecutive string of ones in binary

Given an integer n, return the length of the longest consecutive run of ones in its binary representation.

For example, given 156, which is `10011100` in binary, you should return 3.

Solution

The most straightforward way to solve this would be to loop over the bits of the number, keeping track of a counter of the maximum number of consecutive ones seen. Whenever we see a longer run of set bits, we update our counter.

```
def find_length(n):
    n = bin(n)[2:]
    max_length = current_length = 0

    for digit in n:
        if digit == '1':
            current_length += 1
            max_length = max(max_length, current_length)
        else:
            current_length = 0

    return max_length
```

This is $\mathcal{O}(n)$, where n is the number of digits in our input. Can we do better?

Let's try using using bit manipulation. In particular, note that if we perform the operation x & x << 1, the longest consecutive run of ones must decrease by one. This is because all but one of the set bits in the original number will correspond to set bits in the shifted number. Using the example in the problem, we can see that the maximum length changes from 3 to 2:

```
              10011100
            & 00111000
              ‾‾‾‾‾‾‾‾
              00011000
```

With this in mind, we can continue to AND our input with a shifted version of itself until we reach 0. The number of times we perform this operation will be our answer.

```
def find_length(n):
    max_length = 0

    while n:
        max_length += 1
        n = n & (n << 1)

    return max_length
```

While the worst case here is the same as above, the number of operations we must perform is now limited to the length of the longest consecutive run.

17.4 Find n^{th} sevenish number

Let's define a "sevenish" number to be one which is either a power of 7, or the sum of unique powers of 7. The first few sevenish numbers are 1, 7, 8, 49, and so on. Create an algorithm to find the nth sevenish number.

Solution

A brute force solution to this problem would involve looking at consecutive integers one at a time and computing whether they are sevenish. Once we've found n of these, we return the last one found. To make this a little more efficient, we can use a helper function to precompute a set of sevenish numbers, by finding the totals of all

CHAPTER 17. BIT MANIPULATION

subsets of the first n powers of 7. This way, checking whether an integer is sevenish is $\mathcal{O}(1)$.

```python
def get_sevenish_numbers(n):
    powers = [7 ** i for i in range(n)]
    totals = {0}

    for p in powers:
        # Use set intersection to accumulate sums of powers.
        totals |= {x + p for x in totals}

    return totals

def nth_sevenish_number(n):
    sevenish_numbers = get_sevenish_numbers(n)

    i = 1
    count, last_sevenish_number = 0, 0

    while count < n:
        if i in sevenish_numbers:
            count += 1
            last_sevenish_number = i
        i += 1

    return last_sevenish_number
```

Still, generating all the subsets of the first n powers of 7 is $\mathcal{O}(2^n)$, and we must use an equivalent amount of space to store these totals.

Often when a problem involves taking powers of numbers, there is a bitwise solution, and this is no exception. Note that when we convert a number to binary, we represent it using the form $x_k \times 2^k + x_{k-1} \times 2^{k-1} + ... + x_0 \times 2^0$. To find unique sums of powers of 7, then, we can imagine that each bit represents a power of 7 instead of 2! Let's look at the first few sevenish numbers to see how this works:

- 001 (1 * 7^0 = 1)
- 010 (1 * 7^1 = 7)

CHAPTER 17. BIT MANIPULATION

- 011 (1 * 7^1 + 1 * 7^0 = 8)
- 100 (1 * 7^2 = 49)
- 101 (1 * 7^2 + 1 * 7^0 = 50)

So the nth sevenish number will be the nth binary number, translated into powers of seven instead of two. This points the way to our solution: we will go through each bit of n, from least to most significant, and check if it is set. If so, we add $7^{\text{bit place}}$ to our total. Once we bitshift through the entire number, we can return the total.

```
def nth_sevenish_number(n):
    answer = 0
    bit_place = 0

    while n:
        if (n & 1):
            answer += 7 ** bit_place

        n >>= 1
        bit_place += 1

    return answer
```

This algorithm is linear in the number of digits in our input and requires only constant space.

18

Randomized Algorithms

A randomized algorithm is one in which there is some element of randomness at play. As a result, the output from each run of a program may not be the same, and we may have to rely on probabilistic guarantees for the result or run time.

In general there are two types of random algorithms, both named aptly after gambling meccas: Las Vegas and Monte Carlo. In a Las Vegas algorithm, you can be sure that the result will be correct, but the run time is potentially infinite (though finite in expectation). A simple example would be rolling a die until you see the number 6, and counting the number of rolls.

On the other hand, a Monte Carlo algorithm is one in which the run time is finite, but the accuracy can only be stated in terms of probability. For example, if we flip a fair coin 5 times, we can say there is a $1 - \frac{1}{2}^5 = 0.96875$ probability we will see at least one head.

When dealing with probabilities, simulating some effect, or selecting an item among many according to a particular distribution, random algorithms are a good choice. Randomness can also show up as part of a larger algorithm, such as quicksort, where the pivot is often randomly selected in order to improve performance.

All common languages offer support for randomness, typically in the form of pseudo-random number generators (PRNGs). In Python, you should be familiar with the random library, which offers the following methods:

```
# Generates a float between 0 and 1
random.random() e.g. # 0.4288890546751146

# Chooses an integer in the range a and b, inclusive
random.randint(a=3, b=5) # 3

# Choose an element in a sequence
random.choice(range(10)) # 6

# Permute the ordering of a sequence
x = [1, 2, 3, 4, 5]
random.shuffle(x) # [4, 5, 3, 1, 2]

# Reset the PRNG so that the result of subsequent runs are identical
random.seed(7)
```

Note that when running this code multiple times, the results will be different, unless a particular seed is set before each operation.

While it is impossible to cover all applications, we will explore a few common instances where randomness crops up in interview questions and apply several techniques that are generally useful.

18.1 Pick random element from infinite stream

Given a stream of elements too large to store in memory, pick a random element from the stream with uniform probability.

Solution

Naively, we could process the stream and store all the elements we encounter in a list. If the size of this list is n, we could then randomly generate a number between 0 and

n and choose the element at that index. The problem with this approach is that it would take $\mathcal{O}(n)$ space, and if the stream is very large this would not fit in memory.

Instead, there is a clever method of solving this using a technique called reservoir sampling. The idea is simple: when examining the ith element in our stream, choose that element with a probability of $\frac{1}{i+1}$. To make the calculations easier, we assume throughout this explanation that our indices start at zero.

We can prove this algorithm works using induction. For the base case, we can see that choosing the first element with a probability of $\frac{1}{1}$ is correct, since there are no other options.

Now suppose that we are facing the ith element, where i > 1, and the previous i - 1 elements have been correctly dealt with. In other words, any element k in [0, i - 1] had a $\frac{1}{i}$ chance of being chosen as the random element.

After the current iteration, we would like each element to have a $\frac{1}{i+1}$ probability of being selected. Note that the chance of having been chosen previously is $\frac{1}{i}$, and the chance of not being swapped for the current element is $1 - \frac{1}{i+1}$. Multiplying these together, we find that our inductive step indeed holds true.

$$\frac{1}{i} \times (1 - \frac{1}{i+1}) = \frac{1}{i+1}$$

This is how the code might look:

```python
import random

def pick(big_stream):
    random_element = None

    for i, e in enumerate(big_stream):
        if random.randint(1, i + 1) == 1:
            random_element = e

    return random_element
```

Since we are only storing a single variable, this only takes up constant space!

18.2 Shuffle deck of cards

Given a function that generates perfectly random integers between 1 and k (inclusive), where k is an integer, write a function that shuffles a deck of cards represented as an array using only swaps.

Hint: Make sure each one of the 52! permutations of the deck is equally likely.

Solution

The most common mistake people make when implementing this shuffle is to use the following procedure:

- Iterate through the array with an index i
- Generate a random index j between 0 and n - 1
- Swap A[i] and A[j]

That code would look something like this:

```
def shuffle(arr):
    n = len(arr)
    for i in range(n):
        j = randint(0, n - 1)
        arr[i], arr[j] = arr[j], arr[i]
    return arr
```

This looks like it would reasonably shuffle the array. However, the issue with this code is that it slightly biases certain outcomes. Consider the array [a, b, c]. At each step i, we have three different possible outcomes, since we can switch the element at

CHAPTER 18. RANDOMIZED ALGORITHMS

i with any other index in the array. Since we swap up to three times, there are $3^3 = 27$ possible (and equally likely) outcomes. But there are only 6 outcomes, and they all need to be equally likely:

- [a, b, c]
- [a, c, b]
- [b, a, c]
- [b, c, a]
- [c, a, b]
- [c, b, a]

6 doesn't divide into 27 evenly, so it must be the case that some outcomes are over-represented. Indeed, if we run this algorithm a million times, we see some skew:

```
(2, 1, 3): 184530
(1, 3, 2): 185055
(3, 2, 1): 148641
(2, 3, 1): 185644
(3, 1, 2): 147995
(1, 2, 3): 148135
```

Recall that we want every permutation to be equally likely: in other words, any element should have a $\frac{1}{n}$ probability of ending up in any spot. Instead, we can do the following:

- Iterate through the array with an index i
- Generate a random index j between i and $n - 1$
- Swap A[i] and A[j]

Why does this generate a uniform distribution? Let's use a loop invariant to prove this.

Our loop invariant will be the following: at each index i of our loop, all indices before i have an equally random probability of holding any element from our array.

Consider $i = 1$. Since we are swapping `A[0]` with an index that spans the entire array, `A[0]` has an equally uniform probability of being any element in the array. So our invariant is true for the base case.

Now assume our loop invariant is true until i and consider the loop at $i + 1$. Then we should calculate the probability of some element ending up at index $i + 1$. That's equal to the probability of not picking that element up until i and then choosing it.

All the remaining prospective elements must not have been picked yet, which means it avoided being picked from 0 to i. That's a probability of:

$$\frac{n-1}{n} \times \frac{n-2}{n-1} \times \ldots \times \frac{n-i-1}{n-i}$$

Finally, we need to actually choose it. Since there are $n - i - 1$ remaining elements to choose from, that's a probability of $\frac{1}{n-i-1}$.

Putting them together, we have a probability of:

$$\frac{n-1}{n} \times \frac{n-2}{n-1} \times \ldots \times \frac{n-i-1}{n-i} \times \frac{1}{n-i-1}$$

Notice that everything beautifully cancels out and we are left with a probability of $\frac{1}{n}$.

Here's what the code looks like:

```python
def shuffle(arr):
    n = len(arr)
    for i in range(n - 1):
```

```
        j = randint(i, n - 1)
        arr[i], arr[j] = arr[j], arr[i]
    return arr
```

P.S. This algorithm is called the Fisher-Yates shuffle.

18.3 Markov chain

A Markov chain can be thought of as a description of how likely some events are to follow others. More mathematically, it describes the probabilities associated with a given state transitioning to any other state.

For example, let's say the transition probabilities are as follows:

```
[
  ('a', 'a', 0.9),
  ('a', 'b', 0.075),
  ('a', 'c', 0.025),
  ('b', 'a', 0.15),
  ('b', 'b', 0.8),
  ('b', 'c', 0.05),
  ('c', 'a', 0.25),
  ('c', 'b', 0.25),
  ('c', 'c', 0.5)
]
```

This indicates that if we begin with state a, after one step there is a 90% chance the state will continue to be a, a 7.5% chance the state will change to b, and a 2.5% chance the state will change to c.

Suppose you are given a starting state `start`, a list of transition probabilities such as the one above, and a number of steps `num_steps`. Run the associated Markov chain starting from `start` for `num_steps` steps and compute the number of times each stated is visited.

One instance of running this particular Markov chain might produce { 'a': 3012, 'b': 1656, 'c': 332 }.

Solution

We need to run the Markov chain and keep counts of each state we visit.

It will be useful to define a `next_state` function that takes in the current state and perhaps the possible transitions and their probabilities. Then we can run our Markov chain, starting with `start`, by running `next_state` the desired number of times while keeping track of the current state. All we have to do then is accumulate each state's counts.

Finally, even though we receive the probabilities as a list of tuples, it will be convenient if we transform the list into a dictionary so that we can look up the possible transitions and their probabilities faster:

```python
from collections import defaultdict
from random import random

def histogram_counts(start, trans_probs, num_steps):
    probs_dict = transform_probs(trans_probs)
    count_histogram = defaultdict(int)
    current_state = start

    for i in range(num_steps):
        count_histogram[current_state] += 1
        next_state_val = next_state(current_state, probs_dict)
        current_state = next_state_val

    return count_histogram


def next_state(current_state, probs_dict):
    r = random()
    for possible_state, probability in probs_dict[current_state].items():
        r -= probability
        if r <= 0:
            return possible_state
```

```python
def transform_probs(trans_probs):
    d = defaultdict(dict)
    for start, end, prob in trans_probs:
        d[start][end] = prob
    return d
```

19

Advanced Algorithms

With the concepts discussed in the previous chapters under your belt, you are well on your way to acing your next coding interview. In general, interviewers are not out to "trick" you: they are testing your knowledge of core data structures and algorithms, and your ability to apply this knowledge in novel situations.

There are cases, however, where more challenging algorithms may come in handy, and indeed there is practically no limit to the complexity of algorithm design. Whole books can be written on subfields such as network optimization, approximation algorithms, computational geometry, and more.

In this chapter, therefore, we aim to showcase a couple of advanced algorithms, both because of their importance in computer science and also to demonstrate the way in which simpler building blocks can be combined to create more specialized procedures.

Our first problem introduces the Rabin-Karp algorithm, which uses a clever hashing tactic to efficiently find patterns in a string. Next, we describe a method for finding an Eulerian cycle in a graph known as Hierholzer's algorithm. Lastly, we work through a question involving A^*, a pathfinding algorithm which uses heuristic function to more optimally choose subsequent steps.

19.1 Rabin-Karp

Given a string and a pattern, find the starting indices of all occurrences of the pattern in the string. For example, given the string "abracadabra" and the pattern "abr", you should return [0, 7].

Solution

One solution would be to traverse the string, comparing the pattern to every slice of the same size. When we find a match, we append the starting index to a list of matches.

In the example above, we would compare "abr" against "abr", "bra", "rac", "aca", and so on. If k is the length of the pattern, we are making up to k comparisons for each slice, so our time complexity is $\mathcal{O}(k \times n)$.

```python
def find_matches(pattern, string):
    matches = []
    k = len(pattern)
    for i in range(len(string) - k + 1):
        if string[i : i + k] == pattern:
            matches.append(i)
    return matches
```

If we could somehow reduce the time it takes to compare the pattern to new slices of the string, we'd be able to make this more efficient. This is the motivation behind using a rolling hash.

To explain this idea, suppose we wanted to match the pattern "cat" against the string "scatter". First let's assign each letter in the alphabet a value: a = 1, b = 2, ..., z = 26. Now let's make a very simple hash function which adds up the values of each letter in the hash. For example, simple_hash("cat") would be 3 + 1 + 20 = 24.

To find our pattern matches, we start by comparing "cat" to "sca".

CHAPTER 19. ADVANCED ALGORITHMS

Since `simple_hash("sca")` = 19 + 3 + 1 = 23, we know we have not found a match, and we can continue. This is where the "rolling" part comes in. Instead of computing the hash value for the next window from scratch, there is a constant-time operation we can do: subtract the value of "s" and add the value of "t". And in fact we find that 23 - value(s) + value(t) = 24, so we have a match!

Continuing in this way, we slide along the string, computing the hash of each slice and comparing it to the pattern hash. If the two values are equal, we check character by character to ensure that there is indeed a match, and add the appropriate index to our result.

```python
def value(letter):
    return ord(letter) - 96

def simple_hash(prev, start, new):
    return prev - value(start) + value(new)

def find_matches(pattern, string):
    matches = []
    k = len(pattern)

    # First get the hash of the pattern.
    pattern_val = 0
    for i, char in enumerate(pattern):
        pattern_val += value(char)

    # Then get the hash of the first k letters of the string.
    hash_val = 0
    for i, char in enumerate(string[:k]):
        hash_val += value(char)

    if pattern_val == hash_val:
        if string[:k] == pattern:
            matches.append(0)

    # Roll the hash over each window of length k.
    for i in range(len(string) - k):
        hash_val = simple_hash(hash_val, string[i], string[i + k])
        if hash_val == pattern_val:
            if string[i + 1 : i + k + 1] == pattern:
                matches.append(i + 1)
```

CHAPTER 19. ADVANCED ALGORITHMS

```
        return matches
```

The problem with this solution, though, is that our hash function is not that good. For example, when we match "abr" against "abracadabra", our pattern will match both "abr" and "bra", requiring us to perform extra string matches.

A more sophisticated rolling hash function is called Rabin-Karp, and a simplified version of it works as follows.

Suppose we have a string of length k. Each letter in the string is first mapped to 1 - 26 as above, then multiplied by a power of 26. The first character is multiplied by 26^{k-1}, the second by 26^{k-2}, and so on, all the way to the kth letter, which is multiplied by 26^0. Finally, we add all these values together to get the hash of the string.

So for example, "cat" will evaluate to 3 * 26^2 + 1 * 26^1 + 21 * 26^0 = 2075.

Now suppose we are sliding a rolling window over the word "cats", and we next want to find the hash value of `ats`. Instead of computing the value from scratch, we carry out the following steps:

- subtract the value of the first letter of the current hash (3 * 26^2)
- multiply the current hash value by 26
- add the value of the last letter in the shifted window (19)

Using these steps, the value of `ats` will be (2075 - 3 * 26^2) * 26 + 19 = 1241.

This works because we are essentially shifting the powers of 26 leftward.

If we replace our simple hash function with the new and improved one, our solution should look like this:

```
def value(letter, power):
    return (26 ** power) * (ord(letter) - 96)
```

```
def rabin_hash(prev, start, new, k):
    return (prev - value(start, k - 1)) * 26 + value(new, 0)

def find_matches(pattern, string):
    matches = []
    k = len(pattern)

    pattern_val = 0
    for i, char in enumerate(pattern):
        pattern_val += value(char, k - i - 1)

    hash_val = 0
    for i, char in enumerate(string[:k]):
        hash_val += value(char, k - i - 1)

    if pattern_val == hash_val:
        if string[:k] == pattern:
            matches.append(0)

    for i in range(len(string) - k):
        hash_val = rabin_hash(hash_val, string[i], string[i + k], k)
        if pattern_val == hash_val:
            if string[i + 1 : i + k + 1] == pattern:
                matches.append(i + 1)

    return matches
```

In the worst case, if our hash function produces many false positives, we will still have to check each substring against the pattern, so this would take $\mathcal{O}(k \times n)$.

Practically, however, we should not see too many false positives. In the average case, since our algorithm takes $O(k)$ to compute the hash of the pattern and the start of the string, and $O(n - k)$ to roll the hash over the rest of the string, our running time should be $\mathcal{O}(n)$.

19.2 Hierholzer's algorithm

For a set of characters C and an integer k, a De Bruijn sequence is a cyclic sequence in which every possible k-length string of characters in C occurs exactly once.

For example, suppose `C = {0, 1}` and `k = 3`. Then our sequence should contain the substrings {`'000'`, `'001'`, `'010'`, `'011'`, `'100'`, `'101'`, `'110'`, `'111'`}, and one possible solution would be 00010111.

Create an algorithm that finds a De Bruijn sequence for a given C and k.

Solution

There is a neat way of solving this problem using a graph representation.

Let every possible string of length $k-1$ of characters in C be vertices. For the example above, these would be 00, 01, 10, and 11. Then each string of length k can be represented as an edge between two vertices that overlap to form it. For example, 000 would be a loop from 00 to itself, whereas 001 would be an edge between 00 and 01.

We can construct this graph like so:

```python
from itertools import product

def make_graph(C, k):
    # Use Cartesian product to get all strings of length k-1.
    vertices = product(C, repeat=k-1)

    edges = {}
    for v in vertices:
        # Create edges between two vertices that overlap properly.
        edges[v] = [v[1:] + char for char in C]

    return edges
```

The graph created would be as follows:

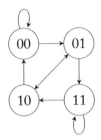

In order to find the De Bruijn sequence, we must traverse each edge exactly once. In other words, we must find an Eulerian cycle. One method to accomplish this is known as Hierholzer's algorithm, which works as follows.

Starting with a given vertex, we move along edges randomly, adding the vertices seen to our path, until we come back to where we started. If this path uses up every edge in our graph, we are done. Otherwise, we can take one of the vertices in our path that has an unused edge, perform the same process on that vertex, and substitute the new path back into the original path to replace the vertex.

We can continue inserting new cycles in this manner until every edge of the graph is used.

For example, suppose we traversed the graph above starting with 01, and found the following path: `01 -> 11 -> 11 -> 10 -> 00 -> 00 -> 01`. Since there is still an unused edge attached to 01, we would next find the path `01 -> 10 -> 01` and substitute it for '01' at the beginning of our original path, resulting in a valid De Bruijn sequence.

```python
def find_eulerian_cycle(graph):
    cycle = []
    start = list(graph)[0]
    before = after = []

    while graph:
        if cycle:
            # Find the next vertex to expand into a cycle.
```

```
            start = next(vertex for vertex in cycle if vertex in graph)
            index = cycle.index(start)
            before = cycle[:index]; after = cycle[index + 1:]

        cycle = [start]
        prev = start

        while True:
            # Keep popping from the graph and appending to the chain
            # until a cycle is formed.
            curr = graph[prev].pop()
            if not graph[prev]:
                graph.pop(prev)

            cycle.append(curr)
            if curr == start:
                break

            prev = curr

        cycle = before + cycle + after

    return cycle
```

Instead of using the vertices, it suffices to return the last element of each one, since that determines the actual path taken. Therefore, our main function should look like this:

```
def debruijn(C, k):
    graph = make_graph(C, k)

    cycle = find_eulerian_cycle(graph)

    sequence = [v[-1] for v in cycle[:-1]]

    return sequence
```

The time required to create the graph will be on the order of the number of edges, which is $|C|^k$. To find the Eulerian cycle, in the best case, we will not need to insert any new paths, so we only need to consider the time needed to pop off and append each edge, which is $\mathcal{O}(E)$. In the worst case, however, we might perform around $\log E$ substitutions, so this algorithm would take closer to $\mathcal{O}(E \log E)$ time.

19.3 A^* search

An 8-puzzle is a game played on a 3×3 board of tiles with the ninth tile missing. The remaining tiles are labeled 1 through 8 but shuffled randomly. Tiles may slide horizontally or vertically into an empty space, but may not be removed from the board.

Design a class to represent the board and find a series of steps to bring the board to the state `[[1, 2, 3], [4, 5, 6], [7, 8, None]]`.

Solution

This is a tough problem to implement in an interview setting, but fear not: we will go through it step by step.

Let's get the challenging part out of the way first: the algorithm. We might first think to use a graph algorithm like Dijkstra's or breadth-first search, but there are some challenges. For one, there are tons of cycles. If we consider a state to be any configuration of digits in the puzzle, it is clear that we can go back and forth between any two adjacent states forever.

Even if we prohibit going back to previous states, moving tiles randomly around the board is extremely inefficient. What we need is an algorithm with the following properties:

- For any given position, we should evaluate successor states and select the best one.
- We should track multiple paths at once, and switch paths if there is a path more promising than the current one.

One algorithm with both of these qualities is A^*.

This is a pathfinding algorithm in which we store all relevant paths in a priority queue, implemented using a heap. With each item we pop from the queue, we:

- Check if the current state matches our goal, in which case we can return the move count and path.

- Find all possible successors to the current state.

- Push each unvisited successor into the heap, along with an updated move count and path.

Crucially, the priority used to push and pop items will be a heuristic which evaluates the closeness of the current state to our goal, plus the number of moves already traveled. This way, shorter paths, as well as those which look more promising, will be selected first.

```python
import heapq

def search(start):
    heap = []
    visited = set()
    heapq.heappush(heap, [start.heuristic, 0, start, ''])

    while heap:
        _, moves, board, path = heapq.heappop(heap)
        if board.tiles == board.goal:
            return moves, path

        visited.add(tuple(board.tiles))
        for successor, direction in board.get_moves():
            if tuple(successor.tiles) not in visited:
                item = [moves + 1 + successor.heuristic, moves + 1,
                        successor, path + direction]
                heapq.heappush(heap, item)

    return None
```

CHAPTER 19. ADVANCED ALGORITHMS

Note that this algorithm will require our board class to store the tiles and the goal state. We also must implement `get_moves`, which finds all valid successor states from a given position.

We will store the tiles as a simple list.

To find the next moves, we first locate the index of the empty square, represented as zero in our list. Next, we examine each of the four ways of swapping a tile vertically or horizontally into this square. If the movement is valid, we add the new board state into the list of successors to return, as well as the direction the tile was moved.

With this logic settled, we can begin to flesh out our class.

```python
class Board:
    def __init__(self, nums, goal='123456780'):
        self.goal = list(map(int, goal))
        self.tiles = nums
        self.empty = self.tiles.index(0)
    ...

    def swap(self, empty, diff):
        tiles = copy(self.tiles)
        tiles[empty], tiles[empty + diff] = \
            tiles[empty + diff], tiles[empty]
        return tiles

    def get_moves(self):
        successors = []
        empty = self.empty

        if empty // 3 > 0:
            successors.append((Board(self.swap(empty, -3)), 'D'))
        if empty // 3 < 2:
            successors.append((Board(self.swap(empty, +3)), 'U'))
        if empty % 3 > 0:
            successors.append((Board(self.swap(empty, -1)), 'R'))
        if empty % 3 < 2:
            successors.append((Board(self.swap(empty, +1)), 'L'))

        return successors
```

```
    ...
```

As you may have noticed above, A^* depends heavily on the quality of the heuristic used. A bad heuristic is not just inefficient; it may doom the algorithm to failure! For this problem, we would like to estimate how close we are to the goal, which is a board that looks like this:

1	2	3
4	5	6
7	8	0

One useful metric we can take advantage of is Manhattan distance. To calculate the Manhattan distance of two items in a grid, we count up the number of horizontal or vertical moves it would take to get from one to the other. Our heuristic will then be the sum of each digit's Manhattan distance to its position in the goal state.

```python
class Board:
    def __init__(self, nums, goal='123456780'):
        self.goal = list(map(int, goal))
        self.tiles = nums
        self.original = copy(self.tiles)
        self.heuristic = self.heuristic()
    ...

    def manhattan(self, a, b):
        a_row, a_col = a // 3, a % 3
        b_row, b_col = b // 3, b % 3
        return abs(a_row - b_row) + abs(a_col - b_col)

    def heuristic(self):
        total = 0
        for digit in range(1, 9):
            total += self.manhattan(self.tiles.index(digit),
                self.goal.index(digit))
        return total
```

CHAPTER 19. ADVANCED ALGORITHMS

Putting it all together, given an arbitrary starting list of numbers, we can first initialize a board class with these numbers, and then use our search algorithm to find an efficient solution.

```python
import heapq
from copy import copy

class Board:
    def __init__(self, nums, goal='123456780'):
        self.goal = list(map(int, goal))
        self.tiles = nums
        self.empty = self.tiles.index(0)
        self.original = copy(self.tiles)
        self.heuristic = self.heuristic()

    def __lt__(self, other):
        return self.heuristic < other.heuristic

    def manhattan(self, a, b):
        a_row, a_col = a // 3, a % 3
        b_row, b_col = b // 3, b % 3
        return abs(a_row - b_row) + abs(a_col - b_col)

    def heuristic(self):
        total = 0
        for digit in range(1, 9):
            total += self.manhattan(self.original.index(digit),
                self.tiles.index(digit))
            total += self.manhattan(self.tiles.index(digit),
                self.goal.index(digit))
        return total

    def swap(self, empty, diff):
        tiles = copy(self.tiles)
        tiles[empty], tiles[empty + diff] = \
            tiles[empty + diff], tiles[empty]
        return tiles

    def get_moves(self):
        successors = []
        empty = self.empty
```

```
                if empty // 3 > 0:
                    successors.append((Board(self.swap(empty, -3)), 'D'))
                if empty // 3 < 2:
                    successors.append((Board(self.swap(empty, +3)), 'U'))
                if empty % 3 > 0:
                    successors.append((Board(self.swap(empty, -1)), 'R'))
                if empty % 3 < 2:
                    successors.append((Board(self.swap(empty, +1)), 'L'))

                return successors

def search(start):
    heap = []
    closed = set()
    heapq.heappush(heap, [start.heuristic, 0, start, ''])

    while heap:
        _, moves, board, path = heapq.heappop(heap)
        if board.tiles == board.goal:
            return moves, path

        closed.add(tuple(board.tiles))
        for successor, direction in board.get_moves():
            if tuple(successor.tiles) not in closed:
                item = [moves + 1 + successor.heuristic, moves + 1,
                        successor, path + direction]
                heapq.heappush(heap, item)

    return float('inf'), None

def solve(nums):
    start = Board(nums)
    count, path = search(start)
    return count, path
```

The running time and space of A^* is $\mathcal{O}(b^d)$ in the worst case, where b is the average number of successors per state, and d is the length of the shortest path solution. Using our heuristic, however, reduces this considerably in practice.

Finally, we should note that up to now we have assumed that a solution always exists, which in fact is not the case. To take an example, we will never be able to permute the following grid to our goal state:

1	2	3
4	5	6
8	7	0

In this case, we will end up evaluating every possible permutation of the board reachable from the starting state, which will be around $O(n!)$, where n is the number of digits.

Part III

Applications

20

Applications

We have up to this point gone through the essentials of data structures and algorithms. If you have worked through each of the preceding problems, you should be confident in your ability to break down any interview problem and find a solution.

In this section we have collected a set of questions which demonstrate the real-world usefulness of the concepts previously introduced. Each one will require you to recognize which algorithm is required and tweak it to meet specific needs.

Fair warning: several of these problems are substantially more difficult than ones in the preceding chapters, and indeed than what you will likely see in an interview setting. Practicing these higher-difficulty questions will help to ensure that you really understand the core concepts, and ideally will make your next interview feel relaxing as a result!

We recommend the following method when working through this chapter's questions, and it applies just as well to an interview setting.

First, read over each problem carefully. Understand what is being asked for, and look for key words that jog your memory of data structures and algorithms from previous chapters. Does a question require finding the top k items? Maybe a heap can be used. Are there overlapping subproblems? Go for dynamic programming.

Next, think through how these data structures or algorithms can be put to use. Sketch out a skeleton of how your code would work at a high level, without writing the implementation of any functions. In an interview setting, this would be a good time to check in with your interviewer to ensure that your structure makes sense.

Once your skeleton code is in place, flesh out the definitions of each function, and adapt the code as necessary to deal with problems that arise. Don't be afraid to alter your approach along the way, but try to figure out why your current implementation isn't working before making any drastic changes.

Of course, you should feel free to refer to the solution if you get stuck. If this happens, we recommend coming back to the problem later and working through it a second (or third!) time, to build up your solving skills.

Best of luck!

20.1 Ghost

Ghost is a two-person word game where players alternate appending letters to a word. The first person who spells out a dictionary word, or creates a prefix for which there is no possible continuation, loses. Here is a sample game:

Turn	Letter
Player 1	g
Player 2	h
Player 1	o
Player 2	s
Player 1	t

Player 1 loses since they spelled "ghost".

Given a dictionary of words, determine the letters the first player should start with, such that with optimal play they cannot lose.

For example, if the dictionary is `["cat", "calf", "dog", "bear"]`, the only winning start letter would be *b*.

CHAPTER 20. APPLICATIONS

Solution

This is a case where using the right data structure gets you most of the way to a solution.

For any set of starting letters, we want to efficiently find out which words can be created later on in the game. In order to achieve this, we should be able to quickly find words that complete a given prefix. This sounds like a perfect use case for a trie. Just like in our chapter on tries, we can build one as follows:

```python
ENDS_HERE = '#'

class Trie:
    def __init__(self, words):
        self._trie = {}
        for word in words:
            self.insert(word)

    def insert(self, text):
        trie = self._trie
        for char in text:
            if char not in trie:
                trie[char] = {}
            trie = trie[char]
        trie[ENDS_HERE] = True

    def find(self, prefix):
        trie = self._trie
        for char in prefix:
            if char in trie:
                trie = trie[char]
            else:
                return None
        return trie
```

When we initialize this trie with the words above, the resulting dictionary will look like this:

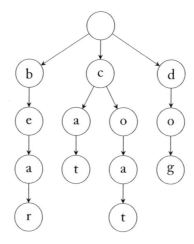

Next, we must figure out what the winning prefixes are. Here, we can work backwards. Any prefix which is itself a word is clearly a losing prefix. Going one step up, if every next letter that can be added to a given prefix creates a loss, then this must be a winning prefix. For example, "do" is losing, since the only continuation is g, which creates a word.

Therefore, we can recursively determine the optimal starting letters by figuring out which ones have only losing children.

```python
def is_winning(trie, prefix):
    root = trie.find(prefix)

    if '#' in root:
        return False
    else:
        next_moves = [prefix + letter for letter in root]
        if any(is_winning(trie, move) for move in next_moves):
            return False
        else:
            return True

def optimal_starting_letters(words):
    trie = Trie(words)
    winners = []

    starts = trie.trie.keys()
    for letter in starts:
```

```
        if is_winning(trie, letter):
            winners.append(letter)

    return winners
```

Constructing the trie will take $\mathcal{O}(n \times k)$ time, where n is the number of words in the dictionary, and k is their average length. To find the optimal first letters, we must traverse each path in the trie, which again takes $\mathcal{O}(n \times k)$. Therefore, this algorithm runs in $\mathcal{O}(n \times k)$ time.

20.2 Connect 4

Connect 4 is a game where opponents take turns dropping red or black discs into a 7×6 vertically suspended grid. The game ends either when one player creates a line of four consecutive discs of their color (horizontally, vertically, or diagonally), or when there are no more spots left in the grid.

Design and implement Connect 4.

Solution

For any design question, it is helpful to spend some time thinking about the structure of our solution before jumping into coding. What are some of the core features of Connect 4, as described above?

- We should represent the board in a way that allows it to change state with each move.
- We should be able to display the board to the user.
- Players should be able to input valid moves.
- We should be able to check whether a win condition has been met.

- To play our game, we should repeatedly display the board, make a move, and check for a win condition.

In an interview setting, it is often useful to create a skeleton of your solution which contains the main methods and how they interact. Here is our skeleton code for Connect 4, then:

```python
class Game:
    def __init__(self):
        self.board = [['.' for _ in range(7)] for _ in range(6)]
        self.game_over = False
        self.winner = None
        self.last_move = None
        self.players = ['x', 'o']
        self.turn = 0

    def play(self):
        while not self.game_over:
            self.print_board()
            self.move(self.players[self.turn])
            self.check_win()

        self.print_outcome()

    def print_board(self):
        # Display the board to the user.
        pass

    def move(self, player):
        # Get and validate input from the user, and update board state.
        pass

    def is_valid(self, move):
        # Make sure the move can be made.
        pass

    def check_win(self):
        # Check for four in a row, and set self.game_over if found.
        pass

    def print_outcome(self):
```

CHAPTER 20. APPLICATIONS

```
        # Congratulate the winner, or declare that there was a tie.
        pass
```

Now that we have a general idea for how to proceed, let's go through each of these methods.

- Printing the board

We will represent our board as a 7×6 matrix, where `board[i][j]` represents the ith row and j^{th} column. Each location in the board can be filled in by an x or an o, representing opposing players. To display the board, we will print out each row one at a time.

```python
def print_board(self):
    for row in self.board:
        print("".join(row))
```

- Making a move

To make a move, we should first ask the user for a column to place a disc in. An input is valid as long as it is a number between 0 and 6, and as long as that column is not already full. Given a valid input, we update the board state and change the turn variable. Note that since discs are dropped vertically into the board, each column will be filled from bottom to top.

Additionally, we will track `last_move` as a class variable, since that will allow us to more efficiently check the win condition.

```python
def move(self, player):
    col = input("{0}'s turn to move: ".format(player))
    while not self.is_valid(col):
        col = input("Move not valid. Please try again: ")
```

CHAPTER 20. APPLICATIONS 244

```
        row, col = 5, int(col)
        while self.board[row][col] != '.':
            row -= 1

        self.board[row][col] = player
        self.turn = 1 - self.turn
        self.last_move = (row, col)

    def is_valid(self, col):
        try:
            col = int(col)
        except ValueError:
            return False
        if 0 <= col <= 6 and self.board[0][col] == '.':
            return True
        else:
            return False
```

- Checking for a win

A naive way of checking for four in a row would be to enumerate all possible lines of four, and for each of these, check to see if all the values are either x or o. We can improve this by noting that if a player has just placed a disc in board[row][col], the only possible wins are those that include that particular row and column.

To make use of this, we will first locate the row, column, positive diagonal, and negative diagonal corresponding to the location of the last played move. For each of these, we will check whether any length-four slice consists entirely of the same player's value, and if so, update the variables game_over and winner.

Finally, we must check if the board is completely full, in which case the game is over regardless of whether or not someone has won.

```
    def check_win(self):
        row, col = self.last_move

        horizontal = self.board[row]
        vertical = [self.board[i][col] for i in range(6)]
```

CHAPTER 20. APPLICATIONS

```python
        neg_offset, pos_offset = col - row, col + row
        neg_diagonal = [row[i + neg_offset] for i, row in
            enumerate(self.board) if 0 <= i + neg_offset <= 6]
        pos_diagonal = [row[-i + pos_offset] for i, row in
            enumerate(self.board) if 0 <= -i + pos_offset <= 6]

        possible_wins = [horizontal, vertical, pos_diagonal, neg_diagonal]
        for p in possible_wins:
            for i in range(len(p) - 3):
                if len(set(p[i : i + 4])) == 1 and p[i] != '.':
                    self.game_over = True
                    self.winner = p[i]
                    break

    if all(self.board[0][col] != '.' for col in range(7)):
        self.game_over = True
```

- The full game

Putting it all together, our code should look something like this:

```python
class Game:
    def __init__(self):
        self.board = [['.' for _ in range(7)] for _ in range(6)]
        self.game_over = False
        self.winner = None
        self.last_move = None
        self.players = ['x', 'o']
        self.turn = 0

    def play(self):
        while not self.game_over:
            self.print_board()
            self.move(self.players[self.turn])
            self.check_win()

        self.print_outcome()

    def print_board(self):
```

```python
        for row in self.board:
            print "".join(row)

    def move(self, player):
        col = input("{0}'s turn to move: ".format(player))
        while not self.is_valid(col):
            col = input("Move not valid. Please try again: ")

        row, col = 5, int(col)
        while self.board[row][col] != '.':
            row -= 1

        self.board[row][col] = player
        self.turn = 1 - self.turn
        self.last_move = (row, col)

    def is_valid(self, col):
        try:
            col = int(col)
        except ValueError:
            return False
        if 0 <= col <= 6 and self.board[0][col] == '.':
            return True
        else:
            return False

    def check_win(self):
        row, col = self.last_move

        horizontal = self.board[row]
        vertical = [self.board[i][col] for i in range(6)]

        neg_offset, pos_offset = col - row, col + row
        neg_diagonal = [row[i + neg_offset] for i, row in
            enumerate(self.board) if 0 <= i + neg_offset <= 6]
        pos_diagonal = [row[-i + pos_offset] for i, row in
            enumerate(self.board) if 0 <= -i + pos_offset <= 6]

        possible_wins = [horizontal, vertical, pos_diagonal, neg_diagonal]
        for p in possible_wins:
            for i in range(len(p) - 3):
                if len(set(p[i : i + 4])) == 1 and p[i] != '.':
                    self.game_over = True
```

```
                self.winner = p[i]
                break

    if all(self.board[0][col] != '.' for col in range(7)):
        self.game_over = True

def print_outcome(self):
    self.print_board()
    if not self.winner:
        print("Game over: it was a draw!")
    else:
        print("Game over: {0} won!".format(self.winner))
```

20.3 Cryptarithmetic

A cryptarithmetic puzzle is a mathematical game where the digits of some numbers are represented by letters, and you must figure out the correct mapping. Each letter represents a unique digit.

For example, a puzzle of the form:

$$
\begin{array}{r}
\text{SEND} \\
+ \text{ MORE} \\
\hline
\text{MONEY}
\end{array}
$$

may have the solution:

```
{'S': 9, 'E': 5, 'N': 6, 'D': 7, 'M': 1, 'O', 0, 'R': 8, 'Y': 2}
```

Given a three-word puzzle like the one above, create an algorithm that finds a solution.

Solution

One way of solving this would be to check every numerical value between 0 and 9 for each character, and return the first character-to-number mapping that works. Assuming it takes $\mathcal{O}(n)$ to validate a mapping, where n is the number of digits in the sum, this would take $\mathcal{O}(n \times 10^k)$, where k is the number of distinct characters.

Instead, we can use backtracking to cut down on the number of possible mappings to check. Recall that for backtracking to be effective, we should be able to construct a partial solution, verify if that partial solution is invalid, and check if the solution is complete. Let's answer each of these in turn.

- Can we construct a partial solution?

Yes, we can assign digits to a subset of our distinct characters. In the problem above, for example, a partial solution might just assign $S = 5$.

- Can we verify if the partial solution is invalid?

Even though we may not know the value of each letter, there are cases where we can disqualify certain solutions. Once we have substituted all the known numbers for letters, we can start with the rightmost column and try to add digits. If we find that column addition results in an incorrect sum, we know the solution will not work. For example, if we had assigned $D = 3$, $E = 2$, and $Y = 8$, our partial solution above would look like the following:

```
    S2N3
+   MOR2
   -----
   MON28
```

No matter what the other characters represent, this cannot work. If the ones column works, we can continue this process, moving leftward across our columns until we

CHAPTER 20. APPLICATIONS

find an incorrect sum, or a character whose value is unknown, at which point we cannot check any further.

```python
def is_valid(letters, words):
    a, b, c = words
    n = len(c)

    carry = 0
    for i in range(n - 1, -1, -1):
        if any(letters[word[i]] is None for word in words):
            return True
        elif letters[a[i]] + letters[b[i]] + carry == letters[c[i]]:
            carry = 0
        elif letters[a[i]] + letters[b[i]] + carry == 10 + letters[c[i]]:
            carry = 1
        else:
            return False

    return True
```

- Can we check if the solution is complete?

Yes, if `is_valid` returns `True`, and we have assigned all letters to numbers, then we have a complete solution.

Therefore, we can implement the solver as a depth-first search, where at each level we take an unassigned letter, assign a digit to it, and check whether the resulting letter map is valid. If it is, we go one step deeper. Otherwise, we try a different digit. If we reach a point where all letters have been assigned and the solution is valid, we return this result.

```python
def solve(letters, unassigned, nums, words):
    if not unassigned:
        if is_valid(letters, words):
            return letters
        else:
            return None
```

```
        char = unassigned[0]
    for num in nums:
        letters[char] = num
        nums.remove(num)

        if is_valid(letters, words):
            solution = solve(letters, unassigned[1:], nums, words)
            if solution:
                return solution

        nums.add(num)
        letters[char] = None

    return False
```

If we chose characters to assign at random, this still would be fairly inefficient. For example, it is not useful to assign $S = 5$ first, because we do not have enough other letters in place to check whether this could be valid. To fix this, we can order our letters by when they appear when carrying out our validity check. We can find this order by going down each column, from right to left, and appending new characters to an ordered dictionary of letters.

```
from collections import OrderedDict

def order_letters(words):
    n = len(words[2])

    letters = OrderedDict()
    for i in range(n - 1, -1, -1):
        for word in words:
            if word[i] not in letters:
                letters[word[i]] = None

    return letters
```

In order for this to work, we must guarantee that each word is the same length. To do so, we can prepend a character that represents 0, such as #, to each of the first two words, until their length is the same as that of the sum.

```
def normalize(word, n):
    diff = n - len(word)
    return ['#'] * diff + word
```

Finally, the code that invokes these functions would be as follows:

```
def cryptanalyze(problem):
    # Input problem is given as [word, word, total]
    words = list(map(list, problem))

    n = len(words[2])
    words[0] = normalize(words[0], n)
    words[1] = normalize(words[1], n)

    letters = order_letters(words)
    unassigned = [letter for letter in letters if letter != '#']
    nums = set(range(0, 10))

    return solve(letters, unassigned, nums, words)
```

To analyze the time complexity, we can look at each function. For is_valid, we check up to three words for each column, so this will be $\mathcal{O}(n)$, where n is the number of letters in the sum. If we let k be the number of distinct characters, then we will call solve $\mathcal{O}(k!)$ times, since each call will reduce the number of characters to solve by one. Since each solve attempt requires a validity check, the overall complexity will be $\mathcal{O}(n \times k!)$.

20.4 Cheapest itinerary

You are given a huge list of airline ticket prices between different cities around the world on a given day. These are all direct flights. Each element in the list has the format (source_city, destination, price).

CHAPTER 20. APPLICATIONS

Consider a user who is willing to take up to k connections to get from their origin city A to their destination B. Find the cheapest fare possible for this journey and print the itinerary.

For example, our traveler wants to go from JFK to LAX with up to 3 connections, and our input flights are as follows:

```
[
    ('JFK', 'ATL', 150),
    ('ATL', 'SFO', 400),
    ('ORD', 'LAX', 200),
    ('LAX', 'DFW', 80),
    ('JFK', 'HKG', 800),
    ('ATL', 'ORD', 90),
    ('JFK', 'LAX', 500),
]
```

Due to some improbably low flight prices, the cheapest itinerary would be JFK -> ATL -> ORD -> LAX, costing $440.

Solution

Let's first think about how we would approach this problem without the constraint of limiting our traveler to k connections. We can think of each location as a vertex on a graph, and flights between them as edges. Considered in this light, our problem is really about finding the shortest path between two vertices. As discussed in the chapter on pathfinding, there are a few ways of achieving this, but one common approach is to use Dijkstra's algorithm.

We will maintain a heap that is keyed on the total cost of the journey so far, and which additionally holds the current node and the accumulated path. Initially, this heap will store a single item representing the fact that it costs nothing to begin at our source airport.

At each step of the process, we pop the lowest cost item off the heap. Then, we take all unvisited connecting airports and place them on the heap, with their accumulated

CHAPTER 20. APPLICATIONS

flight cost and path. Once we reach our destination, we return these values.

To handle the extra constraint, we can add another variable to each heap item representing how many remaining connections are allowed. Initially this will be $k + 1$, and for each flight taken we will decrement by one. If we reach 0, we know that we cannot continue the current path, so we will skip to the next item.

```python
import heapq

from collections import defaultdict

def get_itinerary(flights, source, destination, k):
    prices = defaultdict(dict)

    for u, v, cost in flights:
        prices[u][v] = cost

    path = [source]
    visited = set()
    heap = [(0, source, k + 1, path)]

    while heap:
        visited.add(u)
        cost, u, k, path = heapq.heappop(heap)

        # Stop once we reach our destination.
        if u == destination:
            return cost, path

        # Decrement k with each flight taken.
        if k > 0:
            for v in prices[u]:
                if v not in visited:
                    heapq.heappush(heap,
                        (prices[u][v] + cost, v, k - 1, path + [v])
                    )

    return -1
```

The time complexity of Dijkstra's algorithm is $\mathcal{O}(E + V log V)$. Here, E represents

20.5 Alien dictionary

You come across a dictionary of sorted words in a language you've never seen before. Write a program that returns the correct order of letters in this language.

For example, given `['xww', 'wxyz', 'wxyw', 'ywx', 'ywz']`, you should return `['x', 'z', 'w', 'y']`.

Solution

It may be hard to know where to start with a problem like this, so let's look at the example for some guidance.

Note that from the last two words, `ywx` and `ywz`, we can tell that "x" must come before "z". This is because the first two letters of each word match, and therefore the tiebreaker must be the third letter.

In fact, if we make pairwise comparisons of all the adjacent words in our dictionary, using this same process, we can discover the rest of the rules that govern the ordering of letters. We will store these rules in a graph, where each letter is a key, whose values (if they exist) are letters that must come before it.

Since we compare each letter at most twice, the time complexity of this part is $\mathcal{O}(n)$, where n is the number of characters in our input.

```python
def create_graph(words):
    letters = set(''.join(words))
    graph = {letter: set() for letter in letters}

    for pair in zip(words, words[1:]):
        # Unpack each pair of adjacent words.
```

CHAPTER 20. APPLICATIONS

```
            for before, after in zip(*pair):
                if before != after:
                    graph[after].append(before)
                    break

    return graph
```

For the example above, our graph would be `{'z': {'x'}, 'y': {'w'}, 'x': set(), 'w': {'z', 'x'}}`.

We now want to find a way of combining these rules together. Luckily, there exists a procedure for carrying out just such an operation, called topological sort. As discussed in the chapter on graphs, the idea is that we maintain a to-do list of letters to visit, and only add a letter to this list once all of its prerequisites have been added to the result.

For example, in the dictionary above, we would only add w once we've visited y, so there is no way that y could come before w in the result.

```
from collections import deque

def toposort(graph):
    # Start off our to-do list with all letters without prerequisites.
    todo = deque([letter for letter, prev in graph.items() if not prev])

    # Create a new data structure to map letters to successor letters.
    letter_to_next = defaultdict(list)
    for letter, prevs in graph.items():
        for prev in prevs:
            letter_to_next[prev].append(letter)

    result = []

    while todo:
        letter = todo.popleft()
        result.append(letter)

        # Remove this prereq from all successor courses.
        # If any course now does not have any prereqs, add it to todo.
```

```
            for n in letter_to_next[letter]:
                graph[n].remove(letter)
                if not graph[n]:
                    todo.append(n)

    # Circular dependency
    if len(result) < len(graph):
        return None

    return result
```

Topological sort is $O(V + E)$, where V is the number of letters in the alphabet and E is the number of rules we found earlier. Since neither of these is greater than $O(n)$ (where n is the number of characters in our input), the overall complexity is still $O(n)$.

The glue holding this code together is given below.

```
def alien_letter_order(words):
    graph = create_graph(words)
    return toposort(graph)
```

20.6 Prime numbers

The Sieve of Eratosthenes is an algorithm used to generate all prime numbers smaller than n. The method is to take increasingly larger prime numbers and mark their multiples as composite.

For example, to find all primes less than 100, we would first mark $[4, 6, 8, ...]$ (multiples of two), then $[6, 9, 12, ...]$ (multiples of three), and so on. Once we have done this for all primes less than n, the unmarked numbers that remain will be prime.

Implement this algorithm.

Bonus: Create a generator that produces primes indefinitely (that is, without taking n as an input).

CHAPTER 20. APPLICATIONS

Solution

Despite being very old, the Sieve of Eratosthenes is a fairly efficient method of finding primes. As described above, here is how it could be implemented:

```python
def primes(n):
    is_prime = [False] * 2 + [True] * (n - 1)

    for x in range(2, n):
        if is_prime[x]:
            for i in range(2 * x, n, x):
                is_prime[i] = False

    for i in range(n):
        if is_prime[i]:
            yield i
```

There are a few ways we can improve this. First, note that for any prime number p, the first useful multiple to check is actually p^2, not $2 \times p$. This is because all numbers $2p, 3p, \ldots, i \times p$ where $i < p$ will already have been marked when iterating over the multiples of $2, 3, \ldots, i$ respectively.

As a consequence of this we can make another optimization: since we only care about p^2 and above, there is no need for x to range all the way up to n: we can stop at the square root of n instead.

Taken together, these improvements would look like this:

```python
def primes(n):
    is_prime = [False] * 2 + [True] * (n - 1)

    for x in range(2, int(n ** 0.5)):
        if is_prime[x]:
            for i in range(x ** 2, n, x):
                is_prime[i] = False

    for i in range(n):
```

```
        if is_prime[i]:
            yield i
```

To generate primes without limit we need to rethink our data structure, as we can no longer store a boolean list to represent each number. Instead, we must keep track of the lowest unmarked multiple of each prime, so that when evaluating a new number we can check if it is such a multiple, and mark it as composite. Since we want to keep track of the lowest multiples at any given time, this is an excellent candidate for a heap based solution.

To implement this, we first start a counter at 2 and incrementally move up through the integers. The first time we come across a prime number p, we add it to a min-heap with priority p^2 (using the optimization noted above), and `yield` it. Whenever we come across an integer with this priority, we pop the corresponding key and reinsert it with a new priority equal to the next multiple of p.

For example, for integers between 2 and 10, we would perform the following actions:

Integer	Actions
2	push (4, 2), yield 2
3	push (9, 3), yield 3
4	pop (4, 2), push (6, 2)
5	push (25, 5), yield 5
6	pop (6, 2), push (8, 2)
7	push (49, 7), yield 7
8	pop (8, 2), push (10, 2)
9	pop (9, 3), push (12, 3)

An important thing to note is that at any given time the next composite number will be first in the heap, so it suffices to check and update only the highest-priority element.

```
import heapq

def primes():
```

```
        composite = []
        i = 2

    while True:
        # Note that composite[0][0] is the min element of the heap
        if composite and i == composite[0][0]:
            while composite[0][0] == i:
                multiple, p = heapq.heappop(composite)
                heapq.heappush(composite, [multiple + p, p])
        else:
            heapq.heappush(composite, [i * i, i])
            yield i

        i += 1
```

The time complexity is the same as above, as we are implementing the same algorithm. However, at the point when our algorithm considers an integer n, we will already have popped all the composite numbers less than n from the heap, leaving only multiples of the prime ones. Since there are approximately $n/logn$ primes up to n, the space complexity has been reduced to $\mathcal{O}(n/logn)$.

20.7 Crossword puzzles

A typical American-style crossword puzzle grid is an n x n matrix with black and white squares, which obeys the following rules:

- Every white square must be part of an "across" word and a "down" word.

- No word can be fewer than three letters long.

- Every white square must be reachable from every other white square.

- The grid is rotationally symmetric (for example, the colors of the top left and bottom right squares must match).

Write a program to determine whether a given matrix qualifies as a crossword grid.

Solution

When dealing with a problem with multiple parts, it is a good idea to break apart the task by creating separate functions for every requirement. In this case, we'll define a new function to satisfy each bullet point above.

First, let us determine whether the across and down words all have at least three letters. Note that this will also ensure that each white square is part of two words, since otherwise there would have to be a one-letter word.

For each row in the grid, we will iterate over all words and increment a counter for consecutive white squares. (We assume here that white squares are given as zeroes and black squares are given as ones.) If at any point we encounter a word of length one or two, we return False.

```python
def has_valid_word_length(grid):
    for row in grid:
        word_length = 0

        for square in row:
            if square == 0:
                word_length += 1
            else:
                if 0 < word_length < 3:
                    return False
                word_length = 0

        if 0 < word_length < 3:
            return False

    return True
```

Note this will work for both across and down words, since we can transpose the matrix and reapply on the new grid.

This function will take $\mathcal{O}(n)$ time and $\mathcal{O}(1)$ space to complete, where n is the number of rows in the matrix.

CHAPTER 20. APPLICATIONS

To check rotational symmetry, we need to ensure that the grid looks the same after rotating 180 degrees. While this can be achieved by iterating over the grid square by square, an alternative method is to use a combination of transposals and row reversals.

The following steps will allow us to find the rotated grid:

1. Transpose the matrix
2. Reverse the matrix
3. Transpose the matrix again
4. Reverse the matrix again

Here is how these operations would look on a sample input matrix:

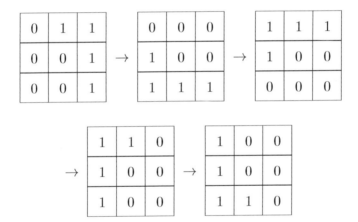

Note that in Python, we can transpose a matrix with the zip operation, by performing list(zip(*grid)), and reverse the rows of a matrix using slice notation with grid[::-1]. The zip operation will change each row into a tuple, so we must map these back to lists at the end.

We can therefore write this operation as follows:

```python
def is_rotationally_symmetric(grid):
    transpose = list(zip(*grid))
```

```
    reverse = transpose[::-1]
    transpose = list(zip(*grid))
    reverse = transpose[::-1]

    return grid == list(map(list, reverse))
```

This operation takes $\mathcal{O}(n^2)$ time and space, since we must iterate over each square and create a new grid.

Finally, we must check the connectedness of our matrix. Recall from our chapter on graphs that breadth-first search is an efficient way of traversing all vertices of a graph. If we think of each grid square as a vertex, then, we can use BFS to check if it is possible to start from a random white square and reach all other white squares.

```
from collections import deque

def is_connected(grid):
    # Check how many white squares there are in the grid.
    count = sum([1 - square for row in grid for square in row])

    # Find the first one to begin our search from.
    start = None
    for i, row in enumerate(grid):
        for j in row:
            if grid[i][j] == 0:
                start = (i, j)
                break

    if not start:
        return False

    # Perform BFS, adding each unvisited adjacent white square to a queue.
    queue = deque([start])
    visited = set()
    connected_count = 0

    while queue:
        square = queue.popleft()
        if square not in visited:
            visited.add(square)
```

CHAPTER 20. APPLICATIONS

```
                connected_count += 1

        i, j = square
        for adj in [(i - 1, j), (i + 1, j), (i, j - 1), (i, j + 1)]:
            row, col = adj
            if (0 <= row < len(grid) and 0 <= col < len(grid) and \
                grid[row][col] == 0):
                queue.append(adj)

    # Check whether the visited count matches the overall count.
    return count == connected_count
```

This function too will have $\mathcal{O}(n^2)$ time and space complexity, as we may iterate over the entire grid and store many of the squares in our queue.

Putting it all together, a valid grid must satisfy all four methods we have just defined.

```
def is_valid(grid):
    return has_valid_word_length(grid) and \
           has_valid_word_length(zip(*grid)) and \
           is_rotationally_symmetric(grid) and \
           is_connected(grid)
```

The overall time and space complexity of our solution will be $\mathcal{O}(n^2)$, since this is the upper bound for each of our component functions.

20.8 UTF-8 encodings

UTF-8 is a character encoding that maps each symbol to one, two, three, or four bytes.

For example, the Euro sign, €, corresponds to the three bytes `11100010 10000010 10101100`. The rules for mapping characters are as follows:

- For a single-byte character, the first bit must be zero.

- For an `n-byte` character, the first byte starts with n ones and a zero. The other n - 1 bytes all start with 10.

Visually, this can be represented as follows.

Bytes	Byte format
1	`0xxxxxxx`
2	`110xxxxx 10xxxxxx`
3	`1110xxxx 10xxxxxx 10xxxxxx`
4	`11110xxx 10xxxxxx 10xxxxxx 10xxxxxx`

Write a program that takes in an array of integers representing byte values, and returns whether it is a valid UTF-8 encoding.

Solution

Note that for an encoding to be valid, the number of prefix ones in the first byte must match the number of remaining bytes, and each of those remaining bytes must begin with 10.

Therefore, we can divide our algorithm into two parts. To start, we check the first element of our input to determine how many remaining bytes there should be, and initialize a counter with that value. Next, we loop through each additional byte. If the byte starts with `10`, we decrement our counter; if not, we can return `False` immediately.

Since we are dealing with bytes, we may find bit manipulation operations useful. In particular, we can perform bit shifts to check the number of starting ones in each byte.

If at the end of our loop, the counter equals zero, we will know our encoding is valid.

```python
def valid(data):
    first = data[0]
```

```python
    if first >> 7 == 0:
        count = 0
    elif first >> 5 == 0b110:
        count = 1
    elif first >> 4 == 0b1110:
        count = 2
    elif first >> 3 == 0b11110:
        count = 3
    else:
        return False

    for byte in data[1:]:
        if byte >> 6 == 0b10:
            count -= 1
        else:
            return False

    return count == 0
```

This algorithm is $\mathcal{O}(n)$ in the number of bytes, since we are only performing performing bit shifts and equality checks on each one.

20.9 Blackjack

Blackjack is a two player card game whose rules are as follows:

- The player and then the dealer are each given two cards.

- The player can then "hit", or ask for arbitrarily many additional cards, so long as his or her total does not exceed 21.

- The dealer must then hit if his or her total is 16 or lower, otherwise pass.

- Finally, the two compare totals, and the one with the greatest sum not exceeding 21 is the winner.

For this problem, we simplify the card values to be as follows: each card between 2 and 10 counts as their face value, face cards count as 10, and aces count as 1.

CHAPTER 20. APPLICATIONS 266

Given perfect knowledge of the sequence of cards in the deck, implement a blackjack solver that maximizes the player's score (that is, wins minus losses).

Solution

Dynamic programming provides an elegant solution to this problem, but it is not trivial to implement.

We can think about the problem like this: suppose we start with a fresh deck of cards, and we deal out two cards each to the player and the dealer. At the end of the hand, the player may have hit twice, and the dealer may have hit once, so that in total 7 cards have been dealt. If we already know the best score the player can obtain starting with the 8th card of the deck, then the overall score for this play can be expressed as `value(play) + best_scores[8]`.

In fact, this hand may have been played differently- neither player may have hit, or both may have hit five times, so that the number of cards dealt may have been anywhere between 4 and 52. Each of these outcomes can be considered subproblems of our original problem that begin with an alternate starting index. If all these subproblems have been solved (that is, `best_scores[n]` is known for all n > start), we can find the best score of any play beginning at start with the following logic:

```
scores = []

for play in plays:
    scores.append(value(play) + best_scores[start + cards_used(play)])

best_score = max(scores)
```

So our dynamic programming approach will be as follows. For each starting index of the deck, beginning with the fourth-to-last card and going back to the first card:

- Simulate all the possible ways that a round of blackjack starting with that card can be played.

CHAPTER 20. APPLICATIONS

- For each play, compute its value (1 for wins, 0 for ties, and −1 for losses), and track the number of cards used.

- Set the value of best_scores[start] to be the result of the logic above.

Once we have our algorithm in place, we just need to add boilerplate code to represent the deck and the players, and to flesh out the logic for how the game is played.

In particular, Deck will be a class that starts with 52 randomly shuffled cards and can deal out n cards beginning at a specified start index. The Player class will be initialized with two starting cards, and will hold cards in a hand that can be appended to and summed up.

The full implementation can be found below.

```python
import random

class Deck:
    def __init__(self, seed=None):
        self.cards = [i for i in range(1, 10)] * 4 + [10] * 16
        random.seed(seed)
        random.shuffle(self.cards)

    def deal(self, start, n):
        return self.cards[start:start + n]

class Player:
    def __init__(self, hand):
        self.hand = hand
        self.total = 0

    def deal(self, cards):
        self.hand.extend(cards)
        self.total = sum(self.hand)

def cmp(x, y):
    return (x > y) - (x < y)

def play(deck, start, scores):
    player = Player(deck.deal(start, 2))
    dealer = Player(deck.deal(start + 2, 2))
```

```
    results = []

    # The player can hit as many times as there are cards left.
    for i in range(49 - start):
        count = start + 4
        player.deal(deck.deal(count, i))
        count += i

        # Once a player busts, there is no point in exploring further
        # hits, so we skip to evaluation.
        if player.total > 21:
            results.append((-1, count))
            break

        # The dealer responds deterministically, only hitting if below 17.
        while dealer.total < 17 and count < 52:
            dealer.deal(deck.deal(count, 1))
            count += 1

        # If the dealer busts, the player wins.
        # Otherwise, compare their totals.
        if dealer.total > 21:
            results.append((1, count))
        else:
            results.append((cmp(player.total, dealer.total), count))

    options = []
    for score, next_start in results:
        options.append(
            score + scores[next_start] if next_start <= 48 else score
        )

    scores[start] = max(options)

def blackjack(seed=None):
    deck = Deck(seed)
    scores = [0 for _ in range(52)]

    for start in range(48, -1, -1):
        play(deck, start, scores)
```

```
        return scores[0]
```

We have n overlapping subproblems corresponding to each starting index, and for each of these the player can hit $\mathcal{O}(n)$ times, in response to which the dealer can hit $\mathcal{O}(n)$ times. This leads to a complexity of $\mathcal{O}(n^3)$.

In reality, neither the player nor the dealer will actually able to hit n times- after holding a hand of all four aces, twos, threes, and fours, the next card would put them over 21. Further, the distribution of low cards in the deck would make it impossible for a player to hit 10 times near both the start and the end of the deck. But for the purposes of an interview question, this is more than sufficient.

Part IV

Design

21

Data Structure Design

One final question type you should be prepared for is design. You can know all the data structures and algorithms in the world, but if you cannot think through how to put together a system that solves user needs or makes a product work properly, this knowledge cannot be put to good use.

On the plus side, design questions usually do not have one "right" answer: the key is being able to identify obstacles, develop a plan to solve them, and examine the tradeoffs between different approaches. In the problems that follow we will address different possibilities in order to illustrate how to work through each situation.

In this chapter we introduce several problems where the goal is to design a data structure that satisfies specific criteria. As in a typical interview setting, these are given in terms of class methods your data structure is required to support, often with time and space complexity guarantees.

In the following chapter we move on to system design questions, in which the goal is to describe at a high level the design of an application or process.

After reading through each problem, we recommend that you consider various changes that can be made to the input requirements, or related questions that could be asked, and think about how your implementation would change as a result.

21.1 Dictionary with time key

Write a map implementation with a `get` function that lets you retrieve the value of a key at a particular time.

It should contain the following methods:

- `set(key, value, time)`: sets key to value for t = time.
- `get(key, time)`: gets the key at t = time.

If we set a key at a particular time, our map should maintain that value forever, or until it gets reset at a later time. As a result, when we get a key at a particular time, it should return the value that was set for that key most recently.

Consider the following examples:

```
d.set(1, 1, 0) # set key 1 to value 1 at time 0
d.set(1, 2, 2) # set key 1 to value 2 at time 2
d.get(1, 1) # get key 1 at time 1 should be 1
d.get(1, 3) # get key 1 at time 3 should be 2
```

```
d.set(1, 1, 5) # set key 1 to value 1 at time 5
d.get(1, 0) # get key 1 at time 0 should be null
d.get(1, 10) # get key 1 at time 10 should be 1
```

```
d.set(1, 1, 0) # set key 1 to value 1 at time 0
d.set(1, 2, 0) # set key 1 to value 2 at time 0
d.get(1, 0) # get key 1 at time 0 should be 2
```

Solution

One possible way to solve this question is using a map of maps, where each key has its own hash table of time-value pairs. That would resemble the following:

CHAPTER 21. DATA STRUCTURE DESIGN

```
{
    key: {
        time: value,
        time: value,
        ...
    },
    key: {
        time: value,
        time: value,
        ...
    },
    ...
}
```

If a particular time does not exist in the time-value map, we must be able to get the value of the nearest previous time (or return null if it doesn't have one). A sorted map would be nice in this situation, but unfortunately Python's standard library doesn't have one. Instead, for each key's inner hash table, we can use binary search to maintain a sorted list of time keys.

```python
import bisect

class TimeMap:
    def __init__(self):
        self.map = dict()
        self.sorted_keys_cache = None

    def get(self, key):
        value = self.map.get(key)
        if value is not None:
            return value

        if self.sorted_keys_cache is None:
            self.sorted_keys_cache = sorted(self.map.keys())

        # Find the nearest previous time key that has been set.
        # If it exists, return the corresponding value.
        index = bisect.bisect_left(self.sorted_keys_cache, key)
```

```
            if index == 0:
                return None
            else:
                return self.map.get(self.sorted_keys_cache[index - 1])

        def set(self, key, value):
            self.sorted_keys_cache = None
            self.map[key] = value
```

The downside of this solution is that each time we perform a write operation with set, we wipe the key's cache, causing a full sort of the keys on the next get call. For write-heavy applications, this would mean most of our calls would take $\mathcal{O}(n \log n)$ time.

For mixed workloads, a more suitable approach is to use arrays under the hood. More specifically, we can store each key and value as corresponding elements in two separate arrays. For example, the value for keys[3] can be found at values[3].

This way, inserting a new key will amount to performing binary search to find the correct index, and then performing two insertions. Meanwhile, each get operation will require a binary search to find the appropriate value index.

```
import bisect

class TimeMap:
    def __init__(self):
        self.keys = []
        self.values = []

    def get(self, key):
        if self.keys is None:
            return None

        i = bisect.bisect_left(self.keys, key)

        # If this exact time is a key, return the corresponding value.
        if len(self.keys) > i and self.keys[i] == key:
            return self.values[i]
```

CHAPTER 21. DATA STRUCTURE DESIGN 277

```
            # If this time is less than any previous time, there is no value.
            elif i == 0:
                return None

            # Otherwise, return the value associated with the latest time.
            else:
                return self.values[i - 1]

    def set(self, key, value):
        i = bisect.bisect_left(self.keys, key)

        # If this time exceeds any previous time, add a new key-value pair.
        if len(self.keys) == i:
            self.keys.append(key)
            self.values.append(value)

        # If this time already exists, overwrite the corresponding value.
        elif self.keys[i] == key:
            self.values[i] = value

        # Otherwise, insert a key-value pair at the appropriate indices.
        else:
            self.keys.insert(i + 1, key)
            self.values.insert(i + 1, value)
```

In this way, both get and set behave more predictably from a performance standpoint. The time complexity of get will be logarithmic due to binary search, and set will be $\mathcal{O}(n)$ in the worst case due to two array reallocations.

The last missing part to solve this question is the top level map. Each time we encounter a new key, we initialize a TimeMap to store its time-value pairs, and use the operations defined above to store and update that data.

```
from collections import defaultdict

class MultiTimeMap:
    def __init__(self):
        self.map = defaultdict(TimeMap)

    def set(self, key, value, time):
```

```
            self.map[key].set(time, value)

    def get(self, key, time):
        time_map = self.map.get(key)
        if time_map is None:
            return None
        else:
            return time_map.get(time)
```

21.2 Queue with fixed-length array

Implement a queue using a set of fixed-length arrays.

The queue should support enqueue, dequeue, and `get_size` operations.

Solution

It may be difficult to know where to begin with a problem like this. Do we try implementing one of the operations? Draw some diagrams to think through how we might add and remove elements?

These are both good ideas, but often a good first step when building new data structures is to think of a simpler structure we can build upon. In this case, let's imagine we only need to use a single fixed-size array, to implement a queue with a maximum length.

In this data structure, we should be able to enqueue up to n elements, at which point our queue will become full. We must then dequeue elements from the front in order to make space. A neat trick when implementing this will be to use a circular array to store our elements. Each time we enqueue an element, we will shift a `tail` pointer right by one. Meanwhile, each time we dequeue an element, we will shift a `head` pointer right by one.

Crucially, we will allow these shifts to circle round to the front of the array. To illustrate this process, let's look at the table below, which describes a series of operations

CHAPTER 21. DATA STRUCTURE DESIGN

on a queue of fixed length three.

Last operation	Array	Head index	Tail index	Size
enqueue(2)	[1, 2, None]	0	2	2
enqueue(3)	[1, 2, 3]	0	0	3
dequeue()	[1, 2, 3]	1	0	2
dequeue()	[1, 2, 3]	2	0	1
enqueue(4)	[4, 2, 3]	2	1	2

First, we enqueue 2 to an array that already contains one enqueued item. At this point our head index remains unchanged, and our tail index has shifted to point to the last element. When we enqueue another element, our tail has no room left, so it circles around to the front of the array.

Each of the two times we dequeue, we return the element located at the head index, and shift that index right by one. Finally, when we enqueue one last time, we can overwrite the value at our tail location, since we know it has already been dequeued.

Here is how this would look in code:

```python
class Queue:
    def __init__(self, n):
        self.array_size = n
        self.array = [None] * n

        self.head = 0
        self.tail = 0
        self.size = 0

    def enqueue(self, x):
        if self.size == self.array_size:
            print('Queue full, cannot enqueue.')
            return

        self.array[self.tail] = x
        self.tail = (self.tail + 1) % self.array_size
        self.size += 1

    def dequeue(self):
```

```
        if self.size == 0:
            print('Cannot dequeue from empty queue.')
            return
        
        result = self.array[self.head]
        
        self.head = (self.head + 1) % self.array_size
        self.size -= 1
        
        return result
    
    def get_size(self):
        return self.size
```

This is fairly close to what we are looking for, except now we must support an arbitrary number of fixed-length arrays. Instead of limiting our queue size, we should start filling up a new array when the current one is full. As for dequeuing, we can still shift our head pointer right each time. However, once we get to the end of our array, we can simply remove that array from consideration, since it will never be useful again.

To help us perform these operations we will track two new variables, the `head_array` and the `tail_array`. The head array will refer to the first list of elements, and will always be what we dequeue from. The tail array will consist of all the arrays, including the head, and will always be what we enqueue onto.

To understand how this arrays work, we can take a look at the following diagram, similar to the one given previously.

Last operation	Head array	Tail array
enqueue(2)	[1, 2, None]	[[1, 2, None]]
enqueue(3)	[1, 2, 3]	[[1, 2, 3]]
enqueue(4)	[1, 2, 3]	[[1, 2, 3], [4, None, None]]
dequeue()	[1, 2, 3]	[[1, 2, 3], [4, None, None]]
dequeue()	[1, 2, 3]	[[1, 2, 3], [4, None, None]]
dequeue()	[4, None, None]	[[4, None, None]]
enqueue(5)	[4, 5, None]	[[4, 5, None]]

CHAPTER 21. DATA STRUCTURE DESIGN

Here, we first enqueue two items to the queue, populating both the head and tail arrays. When we enqueue our next item, there is no room in our existing array for it, so we declare a new list and place this as its first element.

We then dequeue from the head array until there is nothing left to take. At this point, the first array is useless, so we remove it and reassign the head array to the first list of the tail.

As before, each time we add or remove an element, we update a `size` parameter, so that getting the length of our queue is a painless process.

```python
class Queue:
    def __init__(self, n):
        self.array_size = n
        self.head_array = [None] * n
        self.tail_array = [self.head_array]
        self.curr_array = 0

        self.head = 0
        self.tail = 0
        self.size = 0

    def enqueue(self, x):
        self.tail_array[self.curr_array][self.tail] = x

        if self.tail == self.array_size - 1:
            self.tail_array.append([None] * self.array_size)
            self.curr_array += 1

        self.tail = (self.tail + 1) % self.array_size
        self.size += 1

    def dequeue(self):
        if self.size == 0:
            print('Cannot dequeue from empty queue.')
            return

        result = self.head_array[self.head]

        if self.head == self.array_size - 1:
            self.head_array = self.tail_array[1]
```

```
            self.tail_array = self.tail_array[1:]
            self.curr_array -= 1

        self.head = (self.head + 1) % self.array_size
        self.size -= 1

        return result

    def get_size(self):
        return self.size
```

Let the fixed length of each array be n. Then most of our enqueue operations will take $\mathcal{O}(1)$ time, but every once in a while we will need to append a new list to our tail array, which takes $\mathcal{O}(n)$. Since performing an $\mathcal{O}(n)$ process every n steps will lead to a constant time method on average, our amortized time complexity is still constant.

Similarly, dequeuing takes $\mathcal{O}(1)$ most of the time, except for the cases where we must reassign the head and tail arrays. Since this only happens once every n operations, this will run in constant time on average.

The space required for this data structure depends on the number of elements we plan to store. In particular, our space complexity will be $\mathcal{O}(k)$, where k is the greatest size of our queue at any given time.

21.3 Quack

A quack is a data structure combining properties of both stacks and queues. It can be viewed as a list of elements written left to right such that three operations are possible:

- push(x): add a new item x to the left end of the list

- pop(): remove and return the item on the left end of the list

- pull(): remove the item on the right end of the list.

CHAPTER 21. DATA STRUCTURE DESIGN

Implement a quack using three stacks and $\mathcal{O}(1)$ additional memory, so that the amortized time for any push, pop, or pull operation is $\mathcal{O}(1)$.

Solution

Recall that a stack is a last-in first-out (LIFO) container of elements. Therefore, we can support push(x) and pop() simply by using the same methods provided by a normal stack. In order to support the pull() operation, we need to access the least-recently added item, which requires a data structure that supports first-in first-out (FIFO) access.

We can simulate a deque, or double-ended queue, by using two stacks. One stack represents the left, or front (for push / pop), and the other represents the right, or back (for pull). If we assume both the front and back stacks contain elements in the correct ordering, supporting all three operations is straightforward. We push to the top of the front stack, and *pop* from the same stack. When we call pull, we simply pop from the back stack, assuming we've already reversed the elements correctly.

For example, imagine the integers 1 through 6 being pushed in order. Some configurations might look like this:

Front (Left)	Back (Right)
[4, 5, 6]	[3, 2, 1]
[]	[6, 5, 4, 3, 2, 1]
[1, 2, 3, 4, 5, 6]	[]

When we run out of elements in either stack, operations get tricky. How do we make sure that both stacks are ordered correctly? Recall that we can reverse a stack by using an auxiliary array. We can use the third stack as a buffer stack to move and reverse elements correctly. When we need more elements in the right stack, we'll go ahead and move half of the items over to the left stack. We'll pop half of the left stack into the buffer stack. Then, we pop the remainder into the right stack. Finally, we pop the items from the buffer stack back into the left stack.

CHAPTER 21. DATA STRUCTURE DESIGN

Front (Left)	Back (Right)	Buffer
[1, 2, 3, 4, 5, 6]	[]	[]
[1, 2, 3]	[]	[6, 5, 4]
[]	[3, 2, 1]	[6, 5, 4]
[4, 5, 6]	[3, 2, 1]	[]

When we run out of elements on the left stack, we can perform the same operations in reverse. This re-balancing operation takes time proportional to $\mathcal{O}(n)$. However, since we have guaranteed $\frac{n}{2}$ elements on both stacks, there must be no fewer than $\frac{n}{2}$ push or pop operations between each re-balance. Therefore, we can say that the amortized time for pop and pull are each $\mathcal{O}(1)$. The running time for each push operation is $\mathcal{O}(1)$.

```python
class Quack:
    def __init__(self):
        self.right = []
        self.left = []
        self.buffer = []

    def push(self, x):
        self.left.append(x)

    def pop(self):
        if not self.left and not self.right:
            raise IndexError('pop from empty quack')

        if not self.left:  # Re-balance stacks
            size = len(self.right)
            # Move half of right stack to buffer
            for _ in range(size // 2):
                self.buffer.append(self.right.pop())
            # Move remainder of right to left
            while self.right:
                self.left.append(self.left.pop())
            # Move buffer elements back to right
            while self.buffer:
                self.right.append(self.buffer.pop())

        return self.left.pop()
```

```
    def pull(self):
        if not self.left and not self.right:
            raise IndexError('pull from empty quack')

        if not self.right:   # Re-balance stacks
            size = len(self.left)
            # Move half of left stack to buffer
            for _ in range(size // 2):
                self.buffer.append(self.left.pop())
            # Move remainder of left to right
            while self.left:
                self.right.append(self.left.pop())
            # Move buffer elements back to left
            while self.buffer:
                self.left.append(self.buffer.pop())

        return self.right.pop()
```

22

System Design

System design is a broad term that refers to problems where you are asked to come up with a high-level framework to achieve a particular goal, subject to constraints and tradeoffs. This sounds quite abstract, so let's break down each part of this definition.

- A high-level framework

You will not be expected to have in-depth knowledge of every piece of the application you are describing. In fact, if you have a solid understanding of just one piece of the puzzle, that is often enough.

As for the rest, what your interviewer is looking for is typically a description of the end-to-end process and how it achieves the goal at hand. For an application, for example, it would be sensible to outline parts such as the backend logic, data storage, user interface, and network architecture, as well as the APIs that connect them.

- To achieve a particular goal

Sometimes the goal is given directly in the problem: "reduce load time", or "collect user data". More commonly, you will be told the general purpose of the project, from which you will want to ask clarifying questions to figure out how to proceed. There is no end to questions you can ask here, such as:

- Why is this system being built?
- Who will the clients be?
- How frequently will this system be used?
- What kind of data will we need to store?
- What is the scale of the project?
- How efficient does the application need to be?

It is a good idea to keep clarifying until you have a clear idea of what the end result should look like. At this point you should begin to brainstorm a couple of options about how to proceed.

- Subject to constraints and tradeoffs

After carefully scoping the goal through the questions above, you should have a sense of which objectives have higher priorities than others. For example, if the goal is to design a database, you will want to know if writes are far more prevalent than reads, or vice versa.

Each piece of information you receive from the interviewer helps you decide between competing alternatives, and you should feel free to talk aloud while explaining your design in terms of these tradeoffs.

With this definition in place, we are ready to tackle a few system design questions.

22.1 Crawl Wikipedia

Design a system to crawl and copy all of Wikipedia using a distributed network of machines.

CHAPTER 22. SYSTEM DESIGN

More specifically, suppose your server has access to a set of client machines. Your client machines can execute code you have written to access Wikipedia pages, download and parse their data, and write the results to a database.

Some questions you may want to consider as part of your solution are:

- How will you reach as many pages as possible?

- How can you keep track of pages that have already been visited?

- How will you deal with your client machines being blacklisted?

- How can you update your database when Wikipedia pages are added or updated?

Solution

For any design problem, the first step should be to clarify the requirements. What is the goal of this project? Do we have limited resources? How much error can we tolerate?

To answer these questions, an interviewer will often recommend making reasonable assumptions that help you solve the problem. This will be necessary in our case as well.

We will assume, then, that the number of client machines is sufficiently large that we do not need to worry about a few of them failing, and that each machine has access to a separate database to which it can write webpage data. In addition, let us say that the machines can communicate with the server but not with each other.

It is also necessary to know a little about the structure of Wikipedia. A quick Google search will tell us that English-language Wikipedia has around 50 million pages, of which around 6 million are articles. Each article has links to related articles embedded within the text, which must be extracted as we parse the page.

- **Outline**

Now we are ready to dive into the general approach of our solution. Each client machine, or bot, can be seeded with some initial URLs to crawl, designed to explore different topics. The table of contents page (`https://en.wikipedia.org/wiki/Portal:Contents`) has various categories that we can use for this purpose.

For each article, the bot will download the HTML page data, extract new links, and write the text of the article to its database. The links found will provide us with new pages to crawl, and ideally through this process we will be able to traverse all of Wikipedia.

There are several options for how each database might be structured, but the simplest way would probably be a key value store mapping the URL to a JSON blob. Databases will be separate, and we will assume we can combine all the results together once our scraping phase is complete.

Here is how this would look:

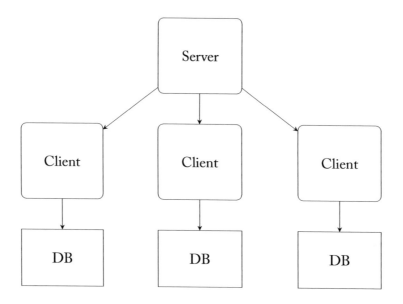

- **Deduplication**

The question now arises of how to prevent our bots from crawling the same page multiple times. For example, it has been calculated that around 97% of the time,

CHAPTER 22. SYSTEM DESIGN

starting from a random page and repeatedly following the first link will eventually lead to the philosophy page.

One solution might be to store a local cache on each client of links already traversed, and only follow links that have not been added to this cache. This essentially amounts to executing n independent breadth-first searches, where n is the number of client machines. However, this does nothing to solve the issue of two clients independently scraping the same page.

Suppose that instead, the server maintains some data structure that keeps track of unique URLs. Before visiting any page, a client will make a call to the server to ensure the page has not been seen yet. After scraping this page, the client will send a second request to the server marking the page as visited.

This is more effective, but at a significant cost of efficiency. A third and improved approach is as follows. Each bot visits and parses its full list of URLs, and populates a set of outward links discovered along the way. This entire list is then batched up and sent to the server. Upon receiving such a batch, the server combines and deduplicates these pages, and sends back the unvisited ones to be crawled.

Our slightly modified diagram is as follows. We only show two client machines for the sake of clarity, but there may be arbitrarily many.

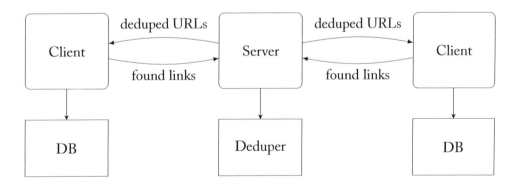

How exactly should our deduper work, though, given that storing every URL in memory may be infeasible? One useful tool we can employ here is a Bloom filter.

As discussed in a previous chapter, a Bloom filter is a space-efficient data structure that tests set membership. At the cost of some potential false positives, we can guarantee a fixed, reasonable upper bound on the cost of checking whether a page has already been visited.

- **Blacklisting**

The advantage of having multiple bots perform our web crawling is that even if a few IPs are blacklisted, the remaining ones can still continue scraping. Nevertheless we would like to avoid this scenario if possible.

First, it helps to follow the rules. Many websites maintain a page called robots.txt, which gives instructions to any bots crawling the site on what pages should be accessed and by whom. We can see Wikipedia's version at https://meta.wikimedia.org/robots.txt. The structure of this page is a series of assignments of the form:

```
User-agent: *
Disallow: /wiki/forbidden_page.html

User-agent: bad_actor
Disallow: /
```

The `User-agent` field defines which bots are being issued an instruction, and the `Disallow` field specifies which domains are off-limits. In the first example above, all bots are told not to visit a particularly forbidden page. In the second, the bot `bad_actor` is told not to crawl at all.

A common reason that bots are disallowed is due to scraping too fast. To prevent this from happening, we can first test the number of requests per second Wikipedia can handle, and throttle our calls to stay within this limit.

It is also a good idea to map client machines to separate kinds of domains. This way, we will not have every bot bombarding the same servers with traffic. In our case, if we wanted to crawl articles in all different language domains, (for example, en.wikipedia.org, es.wikipedia.org, and so on), we could assign pages to each client accordingly.

- **Updates**

Most articles on Wikipedia do not frequently have major updates. However, there are indeed new pages created all the time, and with each news story, scientific discovery, or piece of celebrity gossip, an article probably will be updated.

One simple implementation would be to store each URL and the date it was scraped in a database accessible by the server. Each day we can run a query to find articles older than n days, instruct our client machines to re-crawl them, and update the date column. The downside of this approach is that unless n can be dynamically determined to suit different kinds of articles, we will end up scraping far more (or less) than necessary.

A more sensible approach for keeping track of updates to a site is with an RSS feed, which allows subscribers to receive a stream of changes. In the case of Wikipedia, there are both New Page and Recent Changes RSS feeds. As a result, after our initial scrape is finished, we can direct our server to listen to this feed and send instructions to the client machines to re-crawl the updated pages.

As is often the case in design problems, we have only touched on a few areas in detail, and there are many more questions we could answer. Feel free to explore this in greater depth and implement your own version!

22.2 Design a hit counter

Design and implement a HitCounter class that keeps track of requests (or hits). It should support the following operations:

- record(timestamp): records a hit that happened at timestamp
- total(): returns the total number of hits recorded
- range(lower, upper): returns the number of hits that occurred between timestamps lower and upper (inclusive)

Follow-up: What if our system has limited memory?

Solution

Let's first assume the timestamps in Unix time; that is, integers that represent the number of seconds elapsed since January 1, 1970.

We can naively create a `HitCounter` class by simply using an unsorted list to store all the hits, and implement `range` by querying over each hit one by one:

```
class HitCounter:
    def __init__(self):
        self.hits = []

    def record(self, timestamp):
        self.hits.append(timestamp)

    def total(self):
        return len(self.hits)

    def range(self, lower, upper):
        count = 0
        for hit in self.hits:
            if lower <= hit <= upper:
                count += 1
        return count
```

Here, `record` and `total` would take constant time, but `range` would take $\mathcal{O}(n)$ time.

One improvement we could make here is to use a sorted list or binary search tree to keep track of the hits. That way, `range` would now take $\mathcal{O}(log n)$ time, but so would `record`.

We'll use Python's `bisect` library to maintain sortedness:

```
import bisect

class HitCounter:
    def __init__(self):
        self.hits = []
```

CHAPTER 22. SYSTEM DESIGN 295

```
    def record(self, timestamp):
        bisect.insort_left(self.hits, timestamp)

    def total(self):
        return len(self.hits)

    def range(self, lower, upper):
        left = bisect.bisect_left(self.hits, lower)
        right = bisect.bisect_right(self.hits, upper)
        return right - left
```

This will still take up a lot of space, though — one element for each timestamp.

To address the follow-up question, let's think about possible tradeoffs we can make. One approach here would be to sacrifice accuracy for memory by grouping together timestamps in a coarser granularity, such as minutes or even hours. That means we'll lose some accuracy around the borders but we'd be using up to a constant factor less space.

For our solution, we'll keep track of each group in a tuple where the first item is the timestamp in minutes and the second is the number of hits occurring within that minute.

```
import bisect

from math import floor

class HitCounter:
    def __init__(self):
        self.counter = 0
        self.hits = [] # (timestamp in minutes, # of times)

    def record(self, timestamp):
        self.counter += 1

        minute = floor(timestamp / 60)
        i = bisect.bisect_left([hit[0] for hit in self.hits], minute)
```

```
            if i < len(self.hits) and self.hits[i][0] == minute:
                self.hits[i] = (minute, self.hits[i][1] + 1)
            else:
                self.hits.insert(i, (minute, 1))

    def total(self):
        return self.counter

    def range(self, lower, upper):
        lower_minute = floor(lower / 60)
        upper_minute = floor(upper / 60)
        lower_i = bisect.bisect_left(
            [hit[0] for hit in self.hits], lower_minute
        )
        upper_i = bisect.bisect_right(
            [hit[0] for hit in self.hits], upper_minute
        )

        return sum(self.hits[i][1] for i in range(lower_i, upper_i))
```

22.3 What happens when you visit a URL?

Describe what happens when you type a URL into your browser and press Enter.

Solution

We'll go through a very general and high-level overview of how requests are made, consisting of the following parts: DNS lookup, HTTP request, server handling, and rendering.

- DNS Lookup

First, the URL, or domain name, must be converted into an IP address that the browser can use to send an HTTP request. Each domain name is associated with an IP address, and if the pair has not been saved in the browser's cache, then most browsers will ask the OS to look up (or resolve) the domain for it.

CHAPTER 22. SYSTEM DESIGN

An operating systems usually has default DNS nameservers that it can ask to lookup. These DNS servers are essentially huge lookup tables. If an entry is not found in these nameservers, then it may query other to see if it exists there, and forward the results (and store them in its own cache).

- HTTP Request

Once the browser has the correct IP address, it then sends an HTTP GET request to that IP.

The HTTP request must go through many networking layers (for example, SSL, if it's encrypted). These layers generally serve to protect the integrity of the data and do error correction. For example, the TCP layer handles reliability of the data and orderedness. If packets underneath the TCP layer are corrupted (detected via checksum), the protocol dictates that the request must be resent. If packets arrive in the wrong order, it will reorder them.

In the end, the server will receive a request from the client at the URL specified, along with metadata in the headers and cookies.

- Server Handling

Now the request has been received by some server. Popular server engines are nginx and Apache. What these servers do is handle it accordingly. If the website is static, for example, the server can serve a file from the local file system. More often, though, the request is forwarded to an application running on a web framework such as Django or Ruby on Rails.

These applications eventually return a response to the request, but sometimes they may have to perform some logic to serve it. For example, if you're on Facebook, their servers will parse the request, see that you are logged in, and query their databases and get the data for your Facebook Feed.

- Rendering

Now your browser should have gotten a response to its request, usually in the form of HTML and CSS. HTML and CSS are markup languages that your browser can interpret to load content and style the page. Rendering and laying out HTML/CSS is a very tricky process, and rendering engines have to be very flexible so that an unclosed tag, for example, doesn't crash the page.

The request might also ask to load more resources, such as images, stylesheets, or JavaScript. This makes more requests, and JavaScript may also be used to dynamically alter the page and make requests to the backend.

More and more, web applications these days simply load a bare page containing a JavaScript bundle, which, once executed, fetches content from APIs. The JavaScript application then manipulates the DOM to add the content it loaded.

- **Conclusion**

This is only a brief overview of a possible answer to this question. Any of these topics merit a book-length treatment! Generally, in an interview, this question is asked to see if you're familiar with the web, how it works, and your mental model of it.

It's impossible to know the whole stack in-depth, so sometimes interviewers like to explore a particular aspect of the stack that they are interested in, or you can go into more in depth about a part of the stack that you're more knowledgeable about. In any case, it's interviewers will reward coherent explanations because your interviewers will be working with you and want to see how you think.

Glossary

array 20, 56, 70, 134, 151, 181, 186
backtracking 167, 248
binary search 179, 275
binary search tree 85, 294
bit manipulation 199, 264
breadth-first search 121, 262
depth-first search 121, 167, 249
design 241, 273, 287
dynamic programming 157, 266
graph 119, 189, 224, 254
hash table 30, 63, 140, 274
heap 105, 193, 228, 252, 258
linked list 41, 65
pathfinding 189, 228, 252
queue 52, 122, 129, 278, 283
randomized algorithm 209
recursion 146
sorting 22, 37, 179
stack 51, 147, 283
string 29, 149, 220
tree 73, 124
trie 93, 239

Made in the USA
Lexington, KY
07 March 2019